The
Spectator

THE SPECTATOR

*A World War II Bomber Pilot's Journal
of the Artist as Warrior*

DAVID ZELLMER

Forewords by
Williamson Murray and Sir Michael Howard

PRAEGER

Westport, Connecticut
London

Library of Congress Cataloging-in-Publication Data

Zellmer, David.
    The spectator : a World War II bomber pilot's journal of the
artist as warrior / David Zellmer ; forewords by
Williamson Murray and Sir Michael Howard.
      p.   cm.
    Includes bibliographical references.
    ISBN 0–275–96286–5 (alk. paper)
    1. Zellmer, David. 2. World War, 1939–1945—Aerial operations,
American. 3. World War, 1939–1945—Personal narratives, American.
4. World War, 1939–1945—Campaigns—Pacific Area. 5. Bomber pilots—
United States—Biography. 6. United States. Army Air Forces—
Biography. I. Title.
D790.Z43 1999
940.54'26—dc21
[b]   98–22884

British Library Cataloguing in Publication Data is available.

Library of Congress Catalog Card Number: 98–22884
ISBN: 0–275–96286–5

First published in 1999

Praeger Publishers, 88 Post Road West, Westport, CT 06881
An imprint of Greenwood Publishing Group, Inc.

Printed in the United States of America

The paper used in this book complies with the
Permanent Paper Standard issued by the National
Information Standards Organization (Z39.48–1984).

10 9 8 7 6 5 4 3 2 1

Copyright Acknowledgments

FOR ROSE,
WHO ALSO WORE THE UNIFORM . . .
AND REMEMBERS,
AND FOR DJUNA AND ROBIN

"You describe the sensation of stage when you speak of yourself as Spectator. It is the state of non-feeling in some way that is the highest condition of feeling." (Martha Graham, letter to D.Z., 1/3/44)

"What suits memory best is a war life lived close to the action but at some distance from the values, by a man who is by nature or circumstances an outsider, who can be a witness as well as a soldier, who has felt war but doesn't love it." (Samuel Hynes, *The Soldiers Tale*)

Contents

Photo essay follows page 60

Foreword

They are leaving us now. The veterans of World War II have reached old age; many are in failing health. Even those in the best of health have fading memories of their time, when as young men they had taken history and yanked it back from the abyss of tyranny and horror and opened up possibilities of better tomorrows. In June 1994 a few brave former paratroopers of the 82nd and the 101st Airborne Divisions jumped into Normandy again. Air Force flacks questioned their sanity to want to parachute at their age. But as one of them remarked, "We were crazy then because there were people on the ground who had every intention of killing us; now we are only parachuting."

There are relatively few great works of literature from that war. David Zellmer's creation of a diary of events and reminiscences based the letters that he wrote home to friends, family, and aquaintenances may achieve such status. He has managed to catch in sharp, spartan prose the life of one bomber pilot who flew B-24s in the South Pacific in 1943 and 1944. By so doing, he has given us a window into a period long gone, a period the historical artifacts of which either rest in museums for the viewing pleasures of those who have hardly heard of that great war fifty years ago in what passes for education in America or rot on nameless, forgotten, jungle infested airfields and islands once again at the ends of the earth.

But Zellmer has done more than just describe the combat experiences of one pilot; he has captured the smells of the tropics, the color of clouds and sunsets, the memories of home and those far away, and the loyalties that men engaged in a fierce struggle for survival must cherish. He has

recaptured for our technological age, where all take for granted the experiences, sounds, and sensations of flight, the feelings of another age
where flight, even under the conditions of fear and terror, brought a sense
of awe and beauty to those who flew.

This is also a story of war and the chance that determined some to live
and some to die. The living returned each day to deal with the impersonal
factors that drive great military organizations, but always hanging over
them, like Damocles's sword was an uncertain and ambiguous future
whose line the fates unravelled in days rather than years. Martha Graham,
in whose company he danced before the war interceeded, encouraged Zellmer to write of his participation in the "great tragic play" of World War
II. He has more than lived up to her charge.

Williamson Murray
Harold K. Johnson Professor of Military History,
Army War College

Foreword

This book is an account of a young American bomber pilot's experiences in the South Pacific between November 1943 and November 1944. Perhaps it would be more accurate to describe it as the account of a young American dancer's experiences as a bomber pilot, because David Zellmer's background was as unusual as the events that he described. But first, let us consider the background to those events.

On December 7, 1941, Japan attacked and effectively destroyed the United States fleet at Pearl Harbor, thereby gaining mastery over the entire Western Pacific. She was thus able during the ensuing six months to seize the Philippines from the United States, to destroy British resistance in the Malay peninsula and Singapore, and to gain possession of the oil resources of the Netherlands East Indies (now Indonesia). Penetrating further south into the Solomon Islands and New Guinea, she went on to launch air attacks against the northern coast of Australia, and the West seemed powerless to stop her.

Then in the summer of 1942 the tide began to turn. At the Battle of Midway in July the United States Navy regained command of the Pacific. The following month the United States Marines landed on the island of Guadalcanal at the extreme south-eastern end of the Solomon Islands chain. The immediate object was to safeguard communications between the United States and Australia, where General MacArthur was assembling his forces, but the possession of Guadalcanal would also provide the first stage in a step by step offensive for the reconquest of the Solomons and an eventual return to the Philippines. The Japanese knew this very well, and they fought desperately to keep their hold on the island. Not until the following February were they eventually forced out, after some of the bitterest fighting of the entire war.

When David Zellmer joined his unit on Guadalcanal the following November, the US offensive was well under way. The immediate objective was the Japanese base at Rabaul on the island of New Britain, from which they could dominate the South Pacific. That was the target that Zellmer and his comrades bombed for the next three months; a period during which the US consolidated its hold on the Solomons, thus enabling them, in February 1944, to move west to a base in New Georgia. By the end of that month Rabaul had been effectively isolated, and MacArthur decided to leave it to "wither on the vine" while he prepared a direct assault on the Philippines. Meanwhile Admiral Nimitz's naval forces were driving across the Central Pacific, and from a new base at Los Negros in the Admiralty islands Zellmer found himself attacking the Japanese base on the island of Yap, in preparation for the US landings on Guam, in the Marianas, in July. By August preparations were well under way for the invasion of the Philippines themselves, which Zellmer supported from the insalubrious island of Wakde off the northern coast of New Guinea. In September he moved on to the island of Noemfoor, some 850 miles from Mindanao. From there he supported, but fortunately for him did not take an active part in, an ambitious but disastrous attack on the oil refineries at Balik-papan in Borneo. Three weeks later, on October 20. US forces landed in the Philippines, a few days before Zellmer began his journey home.

This, very baldly, was the operational background to the year that Zell-mer spent flying B-24s in the South Pacific, a period which, like all military experience, combined stretches of stifling boredom with terrifying moments of action. He describes his experiences without understatement or exaggeration, coolly, exactly and vividly. We can see how it was that when he returned to civilian life he abandoned his original profession as a dancer in order to become a writer. But we can also see how the discipline of the dance contributed to his success as an airman—another occupation demanding team-work with meticulous precision. His wartime correspondence with his dance director, the great Martha Graham, must have been unique. He accepted hardship and danger uncomplainingly, and has left a record of his experiences that will be of intense interest, not only to historians of the campaign, but to anyone interested in knowing what it was like to be a young American in the 1940s; how they thought, what they did, how they enjoyed themselves. It was a quite remarkable campaign, and David Zellmer was clearly a quite remarkable young man.

Sir Michael Howard
Robert A. Lovett Professor Emeritus of
Military and Naval History, Yale University

Author's Note

The Spectator chronicles the "deaths and entrances" experienced by a "summer warrior" while flying a B-24 bomber in the South Pacific during World War II. These private moments, known to all, eloquently captured in a poem by Dylan Thomas, and as memorably in a dance by Martha Graham, became my legacy soon after I reported for duty in the Solomon Islands the fall of 1943. In a letter to me on Guadalcanal, Martha warned of these "many little deaths, those moments of doubt, loneliness, fear. Anything. Just any moment when one ceases to be for a short time." She added: "Then there is an entrance again into the real world of energy that is the source of life." She urged me to write about my "deaths and entrances."

I did not, could not, write anything but letters while overseas, needing to reserve all my energy and will, and what Martha called "that complete assembly," for flying. But the letters became, I now realize, a diary of those "deaths and entrances" of which Martha spoke. Many of the letters have now been made available to me and, re-reading them, I can once again live with the tentmates, fly with the crew members I knew so well during those desperate months on the back side of the Pacific. These letters are the inspiration for *The Spectator*.

Perhaps the most truthful letters I wrote, those to Martha Graham, I never got to re-read. But her answers, which I have and continue to ponder, tell me who I once was: A Spectator.

The letters I have been able to re-read were written to the following:

My father, who saved all the dutiful "reports" I sent him, as I knew he would, some outrageously melodramatic and self-serving, but containing "facts" he feared I would otherwise forget or deny. The carefully tied and labeled packet was retrieved following his death.

Geraldine (Babcock) Boone, who was an academic student at Bennington College the summer of 1942 when I was there with the Martha Graham Dance Company for the annual Summer School of the Dance. Our extensive correspondence was personal and special, and the letters were invaluable in my efforts to re-create that alien world in which I then wandered.

Merce Cunningham, the first "real" dancer I knew, to my great surprise and delight, also saved and returned my letters, some detailing forgotten forays along back streets of Noumea, the "Paris-sans-hauteur" of New Caledonia, others surprisingly frank and revealing of my fears and weaknesses as a "warrior." Would that I still had Merce's incisive, cryptic replies, sometimes as confounding as his dance pieces.

Curt Barnard, fellow "Frenisi" crew member, longtime friend and perceptive correspondent, deserves special mention. His dire prophetic pronouncement while both of us were still "out there" that "no one ever really goes home" still haunts me. Curt's memory of those long-ago events is unchallenged.

But of all the letters I received overseas, only those from Martha Graham were saved. Martha once wrote: "A letter is a very special thing, a kind of secret communication that needs no justification or answer . . . something like a soliloquy, as though one were speaking with his secret self, his other face." She added: "But so few letters hit that altitude I keep practically none." All her letters to me during World War II "hit that altitude," and I kept every one. They miraculously survived the jungle heat and rot and constant handling from my re-reading page after page of this catechism for spiritual and artistic survival. The letters are now safe, indeed, at their present depository, the Dance Collection of the New York Public Library for the Performing Arts.

The events described, the combat missions and strikes, have been verified with official sources. The memories and dreams stirred by these letters can never be confirmed, only believed.

My friends of those long-ago days are described pseudononymously to prevent any inadvertent embarrassment. The conversations are my best recollections of words that now seem appropriate to moments only now becoming real again.

Many thanks to Peggy Hafele for her guidance in navigating the world of publishing, and to Roy Howell for his navigation of the maps of the South Pacific.

Finally, special thanks to daughter Djuna for finding someone who not only agreed to read the manuscript but also to publish it, and to her husband, Philip, whose editorial expertise helped make it ready to read.

Warwick, Massachusetts
Winter, 1997

The
Spectator

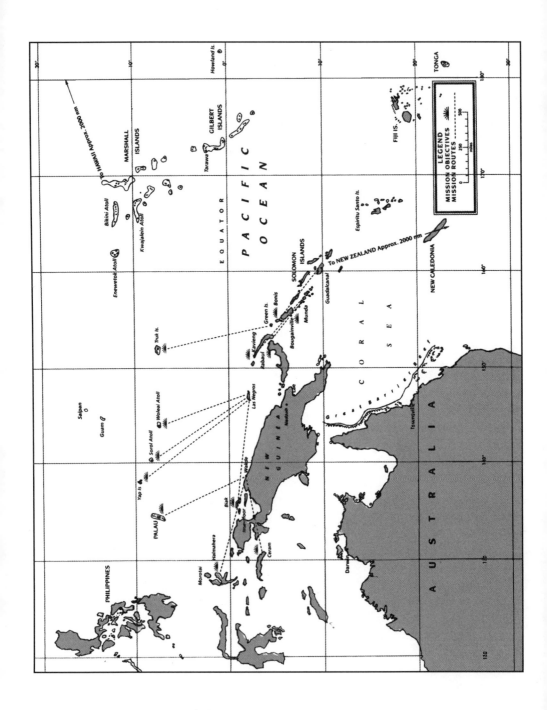

The Spectator

1942

New York City, October 17—It's my last night but one before the Air Force claims me. I'm at the Humphrey-Weidman Dance Studio on West 10th Street in the Village, waiting for the music cue to go on stage in Martha Graham's *Letter to the World*.

I hear Jean speak the familiar opening lines:

> "I'm nobody! Who are you?
> Are you nobody, too?
> Then there's a pair of us."

Then the Party music begins; Frieda brushes my shoulder as she spins out on the stage. I follow as closely as possible and remember to avert my eyes: "You and Frieda must act like a boy and girl who refuse to look at one another even though you like one another very much." So directs Martha at every rehearsal.

Tonight's performance of *Letter* and *American Document* is for a special, private audience: French film director Jean Benoit-Lévy and his staff. He would like to do a film short with Martha, but has not seen these ballets. Martha hopes something can be worked out. She desperately needs the money.

* * *

I quickly change to street clothes during the brief intermission. The girls dress for *Document*; Merce pulls on the Interlocuter costume. Soon, we're all back on stage. The girls surround me and I lean toward them to receive their good-bye kisses and touch their fluttering fingers. A long white silk "aviator's" scarf is draped around my neck. Merce grips my hand; Louis Horst throws me a mock salute. Martha walks with me to the stage door. She holds my hand to her cheek.

The opening chords of Ray Green's score for *Document* ring in my ears as I walk out into the night. I hurry crosstown through the deserted, darkened streets to Penn Station. I board the nearly empty coach of the overnight train to Pittsburgh where I'll say my last good-bye.

Pittsburgh, October 18—My train arrives fifteen minutes before her's from Chicago. We find a room in a small hotel across from the station. Her throat is still sore from yesterday's tonsilectomy, and talking is so painful she writes notes:

"Did Benoit-Lévy like *Letter*? *Document*?"

"Don't know. Left during intermission to catch the train."

"When does the Air Force take you?"

"Tomorrow afternoon."

"Where will you go?"

"Nashville."

"When will I see you again?"

"I really don't know . . ."

I leave when the room begins to darken. Our good-byes are silent and wounding. I hurry to catch the next train back to New York. Her train to Chicago leaves in the morning.

Nashville, October 20—The train arrives here long after dinner time but we're nevertheless marched a mile across the Classification Center grounds to a prophylactic station and short-armed for VD. The sinless among us are then, at long last, escorted to a mess hall for a 10:30 PM meal of hot dogs, beans and corn bread.

Hank and Scotty, my seatmates for the 30-hour train ride from Jersey City, and I are fortuitously assigned to the same barracks. We're already friends despite our disparate backgrounds. I tell them I was involved in

theatre work but do not volunteer specifics. Hank worked for an adver-
tising firm, is knowledgable about the New York business world. Scotty
was a statistician for the British Aircraft Commission and is well informed
on British military affairs. He claims to know with certainty that U.S. Air
Force pilots, like RAF officers, are assigned a personal batman upon being
commissioned. Hank and I do not think so but do not argue with 5'4"-
tall Scotty.

We're agreed that this is a momentous day for us. Our one-size-fits-all
coveralls do not enhance our perceived self-image of fearless fighter pilots,
but we're determined to somehow acknowledge the occasion. We find a
shovel behind the barracks and proceed to dig a large hole in the red
powdery soil and bury our civilian clothes.

1943

Camden, S.C., February 8—What an unlikely setting for an Air Force flying school! Its collection of white-shingled, green-roofed buildings are clustered in a pine grove; the spacious, brightly-lighted mess hall is staffed by white-coated (black) waiters; and we eat off tablecloths and hold cloth napkins on our laps. One of the landing fields is just 50 yards from the barracks where I sleep—and now dream only of flying, no longer of P., not even of the dancer's life I surrendered so reluctantly.

All our instructors are civilians—former airline pilots, crop dusters, barnstormers—mine, whom I share with three other cadets, taught flying, stunt flying, at a small airport outside Atlanta. His name tag reads "C. Johnston," and I shall probably never learn what the "C" stands for.

For the last six weeks, at Maxwell Field, *everyone* we dealt with was named "Sir," all uniformed military types, wearing bars or stripes. It was an unforgiving six weeks of West Point-style academic instruction and basic military drill.

* * *

Today I learned how to do "gliding turns." Our plane is a single-engined PT-17, two wings and two open cockpits. Johnson sits in the forward one and "directs" me, by shouting through the speaking tube, to fly us over to a nearby cloud. Then he takes over. We hesitate momentarily—as a hawk would—to contemplate the descent over the cotton field below. Johnston closes the throttle, pushes the stick forward—we have dual controls, and I follow his every move with my hands and feet—until the nose of the plane is down just below the horizon. We then begin silent, gliding half turns, first to the right, then to the left, back and forth, lazily back and forth, the plane falling lower and lower with each turn, but always staying almost level, like a leaf fluttering down . . . At the last possible moment, dangerously close to the cotton field below, Johnston pulls the nose up and rams the throttle full forward. We soar back up into the sky to find another cloud perch, and I have my turn at doing "gliding turns" . . .

Bush Field, Augusta, Ga., May 1—Today's the half-way point of the pilot training program. In just three months I'll get my wings and commission, if all goes well . . . This second phase of flight training is serious, indeed. (Why is it called "Basic?") Four guys have been killed in the past three weeks—two just last Friday. The plane we use, a Vultee, is very "hot," has twice the horsepower of the little Stearman biplane we flew in Primary. Lands at 90 MPH, and, of course, stalls—falls out of the sky—if one goes slower than 90 MPH. Most aerobatic maneuvers are somewhat too risky to attempt.

I'm now into the night flying stage of training. There's a quarter-moon up this week, making enough light to see the ground below and distinguish open fields from the woods. Roads are easy to follow. It's a quite beautiful scene—like a darkened oriental rug from 1500 feet.

But night before last, a fog suddenly moved in. I could no longer see the airfield lights, and had to fly by instruments only—which I'd never done before. Tower told me to stay at 2000 feet and fly in a large circle—which I did for an hour, praying all the time there were no other planes at 2000 feet. It was long after midnight by the time the fog cleared and I was able to land. Bed, finally, at 3:00 AM.

* * *

I'll go to Turners Field, Albany, Georgia, at the end of the month for Advanced Training in twin-engine planes. I've requested Light Bombers as my first choice of a combat plane. Really wanted a P-38, but at my "advanced age" of 25, I really can't compete with all those "hot-shot" 19-year-olds.

Turners Field, Albany, Ga., July 28—Today I was awarded my Pilot's Wings and, almost incidentally, got commissioned a Second Lieutenant. But not assigned a batman; and Scotty is not here to explain why not: he never made it to Pilot Training—ended up at Bombardier School. Hank was classified a pilot but we lost track of one another after Nashville.

Dad was here, all the way from Wisconsin. Pinned the Wings on; wished me luck "up there." Climbed back aboard a train after dinner for the long ride back to Wisconsin.

While we ate (fried country ham with red-eye gravy, grits and hot biscuits) he asked what made me decide to become a flyer. Said I didn't remember ever "deciding." Once I got classified 1A in the Draft, I simply "knew" I wanted the Air Force. I could "imagine" myself a flyer, not a sailor or soldier. Told him maybe it was because of that 15-minute ride in a barnstorming Ford Tri-Motor plane he arranged for my brother and me when I was 12. The plane landed at the town's little airport for gas one weekend. We happened to be driving by. Dad offered the pilot $5 for a 15-minute ride.

It didn't seem an especially exciting flight at the time: the all-metal plane was noisy and bumpy and very slow. But I loved the view from up there—still remember it: Wisconsin River cutting the town right in half; the long, high dam by the papermill, just above the town swimming pool; cranberry bogs east of town. And the clouds—sometimes even below us—looking solid enough to walk on. For weeks after that flight, brother Rob and I "flew" a plane we fashioned from a turned-over straight-back chair pulled up to the knee-hole of my father's desk. The knee-hole was the cabin or cockpit; we sat in there, under the desk, and steered with the chair legs. Hung a small rug over the chair back: this was the "engine." Rob and I spent hours in that plane.

Dad said he'd forgotten all that. I knew why: my mother died that spring. A lady was hired to take care of us. Rob and I spent a lot of time "flying." Dad spent a lot of time, by himself, in his office at the school.

Tomorrow I go to Maxwell Field, Montgomery, Alabama, for six weeks to learn how to fly a B-24. Will soon find out if the past eight months of flight training "shows."

Hank Walters is going to B-17 school. Hank and I have been roommates all those eight months. The "Ws" and "Zs" are likely to be roommates, or at least "neighbors" in this outfit. It's not guaranteed to produce friendships but I thought Hank and I did have many similar interests. Fewer than I realized. Hank told me today that he's been an FBI "spotter" all the time we've known one another. Said he once almost turned me in because, at the time, I was receiving copies of the magazine *In Fact*, a liberal investigative journal that was on his list of "questionable" magazines. Did not report me when he learned I was only a reader, not a subscriber. "Only" a reader . . .

* * *

Maxwell Field, Montgomery, Ala., October 4—My last cross-country flight from Maxwell completed, I'm now officially a B-24 First Pilot-Airplane Commander. We've finished all classes and will leave for Salt Lake City at the end of the week to await orders. The possibilities are an assignment to the Air Transport Command to ferry troops or deliver planes; or to Davis Monthan in Tucson for six weeks of combat training, then overseas.

Yesterday's cross-country was very special. I got to fly all the way to Wisconsin and "buzz" the Zellmer house on Elm Street in Wisconsin Rapids. Ray and Gerry, who also have Peterson as an instructor, flew us to their hometowns—Ray lives in Pueblo, Colorado, and Chicago was substituted for White Plains, New York, Gerry's hometown, because the entire eastern seaboard was off limits for training flights; and Gerry has a girlfriend in a Chicago suburb.

I found Wisconsin Rapids soon after crossing the Mississippi River into Wisconsin about 50 miles below St. Paul, at a place where the Mississippi widens and looks like a lake—we called it Lake Pepin when I lived in the tiny nearby river town of Alma 20 years ago. We were flying due east, and I began losing altitude, because there, directly ahead, was Wisconsin Rapids, in the center of the state where my grade school geography book said it was.

We're now flying at about 1,000 feet. The scene below is exactly as I remember it from that day in 1930 when brother Rob and I looked down from a Ford Tri-Motor to see the snaking Wisconsin River cutting the town in half . . .

I flew a large, wide circle, over Port Edwards to the south, then directly over the bridge that spans the river in the center of town. I was now at 500 feet. And there, as I knew it would be, unfolding directly ahead, was the field where we played baseball, Witter Field, the private in-town pasture for Mr. Witter's riding horse. The field was bounded on one side by Elm Street, and I caught a glimpse of the house where I once lived. My father was on the back steps, waving. I dipped the wings of the plane and flew on . . .

Davis–Monthan Field, Tucson, Ariz., October 30—I've been here just two days, about to begin the final phase of my bomber pilot training: learn how to drop bombs without being shot down by enemy planes or anti-aircraft guns, among other neat tricks; and get "my" own crew, and a brand-new B-24 to fly overseas. Wherever.

But an hour ago I was hand-delivered special orders telling me I'm one of four pilots selected to be sent overseas next week as a "co-pilot replacement." Instead of taking the combat course. Our destination is not given but the orders say we are to be "equipped for semi-tropical climate."

Almost as unsettling, half an hour ago I was assigned to fly co-pilot tonight for a crew needing six more hours of night instrument flying to finish the combat training course. I, of course, had other plans. Sam and Gino, who are also on the overseas orders, and coincidently my roomates, thought we might do a little celebrating as befits the occasion of unexpectedly being ordered overseas.

I've known Sam since I began pilot training, but only well enough to say "Hi!" to. His last name begins with "W," and we've lived in the same barracks most of that time. He comes from a town just north of New York

City, but has never heard of Greenwich Village, in the City, where I lived. I did not tell him I was a dancer. He did not tell me what he did in civilian life.

Gino was not known by either of us until he moved into our barracks yesterday. He's from Brooklyn, and his last name—Italian—is very similar to that of a well-known mobster family. Sam and I do not pursue the matter.

En Route to Hawaii, November 10—I'm aboard a C-87 bound for Hickam Field and points beyond. There are 19 of us aboard, nearly all newly graduated B-24 pilots. The plane is a transport version of that same bomber we all know so well. The plane's unlike any I've ever flown: red leather padded seats; sound-proof cabin with indirect lighting; and a GI attendant who serves coffee and fruit drinks and sandwiches on request. He tells us we lucked into getting the same plane, No. 558, that Eleanor Roosevelt used last August to visit US troops in Australia

It's not until the Golden Gate Bridge fades from sight that we're permitted to open our sealed travel orders: they say our ultimate destination is a place called "Espiritu Santo," where the 13th Air Force is headquartered. None of us have ever heard of "Espiritu Santo"—or the 13th Air Force.

I have a copy of *Time* magazine, a current issue. I read the war news first: Naples has been taken by the US 5th Army; allied forces have invaded an island in the Solomons called Bougainville. There's a War Map of the South Pacific Theatre, and I quickly find Bougainville. Then I see, to the south of it, the place we all know, Guadalcanal. And there, an inch below Guadalcanal, is our new base, Espiritu Santo, in the New Hebrides Islands. No mention of a 13th Air Force.

I find another story of interest in *Time*. It concerns the trial in Nassau of Count Alfred de Marigny, who's charged with murdering his wealthy father-in-law, Sir Harry Oakes. De Marigny is the husband of Nancy Oakes whom I remember as an occasional student at the Martha Graham Dance Studio. Before she married de Marigny.

And there's a sobering story of a protest demonstration by Japanese-American internees at Tule Lake, California. I think of the Japanese-Americans I know, whose parents and relatives may be at Tule Lake. Will we still be friends when all this is over?

Gino is in the seat next to me. We trade titillating San Francisco memories. Sam is across the aisle, asleep. The three of us have been inseparable since leaving Tucson. We were given a short leave before reporting to the Embarkation Base outside San Francisco. We begin it in Los Angeles, determined to finally see Hollywood before heading out to that "semi-tropical" overseas base: have our pictures snapped at Hollywood and Vine; lunch at the Brown Derby; have a soda at Schwabs Pharmacy; and trace Betty Grable's handprint in the sidewalk in front of Graumans. Sleep somewhat guiltily in a luxurious suite at the palatial Ambassador Hotel, rented to us at a special rate of $14 a night.

When we move on to San Francisco, the even more elegant Palace Hotel also forgives us our awkwardness and antics, undoubtedly in deference to our uniforms and pilot wings, and knowing that these are the remaining days and nights of a reluctant farewell visit.

The final days were spent at Hamilton Field, the Airport of Embarkation, too tantalizingly near the paradise of downtown San Francisco to be executing final wills, assigning pay allotments and submitting to shots for small pox, tetnus, typhoid, typhus and cholera—wasn't time for yellow fever. Most of the equipment I was issued—a glove-leather tight fitting flying helmet, a rubber oxygen mask molded to the contours of my face, a parachute harness, jungle survival kit, blanket roll, pup-tent—went into a footlocker to be shipped by boat. I got to wear the new wristwatch, the .45 pistol in its shoulder holster, and a sheathed 5-inch bladed hunting knife.

* * *

The flight seems endless: ten hours to Hawaii. I stare at the water below: glistening, seamless, an undulating bluegreen seascape spreading to the horizon in all directions. Gino, rather uncharacteristically, is now silent, and closes his eyes. Sam sleeps on. I watch the plane's shadow moving crablike slightly ahead of us. I think of where I'm going, the inevitabilty of combat, the loom of a tragic ending. And of those I've left behind at places I called "home." I redraw all the faces. Then, unexplainably, I'm dreaming back to Camden, in South Carolina, where I learned to fly, remembering the small resort-like flying school, its cluster of green-roofed, white-shingled buildings in a grove of tall pines, the landing strip just 50 yards from the barracks where I slept and dreamt only of flying: of doing gliding turns, the plane losing altitude, falling, fluttering down like a leaf, finally halted in its descent perilously close to the field below; of then soaring back up to another, even higher cloud, to perch again; and now hearing Johnston shout into the tube: "Spin her down! Two turns to the right!" I cower lower in the wind-raked cockpit; cut the throttle; thrust the stick all the way forward; hold it there until the plane's aimed straight down at the same cotton field. I kick right-rudder, hold it there. We begin turning ever so slowly. I peer out over the rim of the cockpit, through the wing struts, the slowly turning propeller. I count the turns of our spin by spotting on a barn in a corner of the field—and remember how I once spotted on a doorknob in Martha's studio while attempting a pirouette. A lifetime ago. . . .

My reverie is interrupted by members of the plane's flight crew entering the cabin to induct all 19 of us into the "Short Snorter Club." We're told it's an honorary society for anyone who has flown over the equator or the international date line. Of course, we've done neither, nor will we until tomorrow, with a different crew. It's soon apparent that this crew means to collect the dollar each of us must pay to join the club. We surrender a second dollar they sign and inscribe with the date and our position: "11/ 10/43 Lat. 34'E & Long. 130'W" We're about 400 miles southwest of San Francisco.

Hickam Field, 9:00 PM—The imagined forbidden pleasures of Honolulu are not to be savored by me this night. Immediately upon landing I learn we are restricted to the base. I'm compelled to watch the city's lights across the bay surreptitiously wink in defiance of the blackout. I bemoan my fate.

The stairwell of the barracks is still scarred by straffing inflicted during the Japanese attack on Pearl Harbor nearly two years ago. I'm sobered by this unexpected reminder of why I'm here.

En Route to Canton Island, November 11—The plane lifts off Hickam's runway shortly after dawn, banks slightly right to avoid entering forbidden air space over Pearl Harbor. Below, Honolulu is slowly emerging from the shadows of the dusk-to-dawn blackout. Punchbowl Crater, soon to become a memorial cemetery for Pacific casualties, is now under the right wing. I nudge Gino and point to it, telling him a gravesite will be reserved there for each of us, just in case . . . Gino shakes his head slowly, then closes his eyes.

The plane continues to climb, slowly turning to find the direction of Canton Island, 2000 miles to the southwest. It's our only fuel stop between here and Fiji: the point of no return . . . I watch a ribbon of surf off Barber's Point catch fire from sparks of the emerging sun.

I close my eyes and dream back to yesterday: the Golden Gate Bridge slowly slipping beneath the shadow of our plane; San Francisco's skyline blurring in the distance. Feeling all ties to that world breaking, one by one . . .

A lone, towering cumulus cloud, glowing in the late afternoon sun, hovers over the tiny speck on the horizon that is our destination, the sea level atoll called Canton. Even as we approach, slowly decreasing our altitude, the island grows to become a giant coral and sand "scimitar." Our plane aims for a slender landing strip running the length of the scimitar's "handle." On the final approach, still a thousand feet above outlying reefs, I see a narrow surf-washed beach immediately to the left of the runway; a large, shimmering lagoon on the other side.

Our steep, powered glide down from the sky abruptly ends with a lurch and squeal of tires and the ker-thump of the nosewheel. There follows a brief 100-mile-an-hour hurtle onward, abruptly slowed, then stopped, with full flaps and stomped brakes.

Someone pushes open the cabin door even before the propellers stop turning. Warm, humid tropical air, tinged with the fetid scent of the sea, pours inside. I step down to the tarmac. My cheeks are stung by salt spray and spun sand swirling towards the lagoon. Petulant gulls circle overhead, screeching their disapproval of our presence. The omnipresent deep-throated roar of airplane engines being revved up is familiar; not the constant thunderous crash of the surf against this tiny atoll.

Refueling completed, I reluctantly climb back aboard. Fiji is 1,200 miles farther on. I've learned during this brief interlude that Canton has no Chinese heritage, that it was named for a New Bedford, Massachusetts, whaling ship wrecked here in the 1800s. I'm persuaded no one has ever called this lost, treeless refuge "home." Certainly no natives live here now.

We're in the air again in time to follow the reluctant descent of the sun, and watch it, under the right wing, slowly slip out of sight at the horizon. There, the red-orange stains of the dying day are briefly reflected, then swallowed.

Nandi Air Base, Vita Luva, Fiji, November 13—This day should be the 12th, but shortly before arriving at this New Zealand Air Base last night, we crossed the international date line and lost a day. We'll get it back on the way home . . . if and when, as they say.

I'm of course now legally eligible to be a member of the Short Snorter Club—doubly so, since we also crossed the Equator yesterday, a couple of hours before landing on Canton Island.

There's a 24-hour layover here for routine maintenance on the plane, but I'll see nothing of Fiji: we're restricted to the base, meaning the Officers Club, which, alas, is closed for bar business and quite deserted during daytime hours. The only native Fijians I've seen, or am likely to encounter, are the waiters and the non-serving bartender. The bartender is a huge, no-nonsense type, jet black, frizzy-haired, white-coated and barefoot. He sold me a carton of Chesterfields for 50¢ but only after I agreed to also buy a carton each of Players and Wings. "Regulations," he solemnly intoned to explain the tie-in sales practice.

We fly to Nouméa, New Caledonia, in the morning, a five-hour flight to the southwest. The city is said to be "wide open" and French, a promising combination.

Tontouta Airport, Nouméa, November 14—I had only a brief aerial glimpse of Nouméa as we circled to land this afternoon: a cityscape of red and blue roofs mounted on a quilt of crisscrossed leaf-shaded streets radiating from a central square. Sliding beneath our left wing was a land-locked harbor, its surface crowded with tethered green-and-black camouflaged ships.

When this same plane landed here with Eleanor Roosevelt, three months ago, an American General and an Australian Colonel were waiting with a chauffeured limousine to drive her to a dinner hosted by an Admiral William "Bull" Halsey. When we landed today, a PFC was waiting with a 6×6 open-bed truck to take us and our baggage to the Transient Officers mess hall where we paid 10¢ each for an unhosted, totally dehydrated dinner. The anti-malaria pills were free. We had arrived too late from Fiji to catch the last truck-shuttle into Nouméa, and the only alternative was the movie. Hollywood could not have designed a more impressive setting for seeing *Watch on the Rhine*: the huge screen was erected in a natural amphitheatre formed by hills surrounding Tontouta. I watched in awe as hundreds of men slowly moved up the darkened slope to the rim of the "bowl," silhouetted by the largest full moon I have ever seen, then descended in shadowy waves to the acres of low, plank benches. A song everyone knew, *Sunday, Monday and Always*, spilled from the loudspeakers as we waited for the picture to begin. Watching the film, I felt I needed no excuse to laugh or cry—but did neither. I did forget, for an hour or so, where I was.

Nouméa, November 15—One reaches this exotic French city from Tontouta Airport by means of a 30-mile, perilous ride down a steep mountain road full of hairpin turns, at the bottom of which sits a large American cemetery bristling with rows of white crosses marking graves of, not combat soldiers, but truck drivers who failed to negotiate one of the turns.

This is certainly a "French" city to judge by the shop signs and the chatter one hears on the street. It is made to seem even more exotic by the presence of hundreds of Asians. These Vietnamese, Indonesians, Indians, all in colorful native dress, I soon learned, are indentured laborers in the country's vast nickel mines, now stranded thousands of miles from their homes by the war.

The sun-baked downtown streets are flanked by open sewers which tempt dogs and small children alike, and convince us that the Officers Club is the only "safe" place to eat. Unfortunately, the cuisine there is strictly GI. Only the fries are French.

In residential areas, the tree-shaded streets are lined with stately old mansions, built by the French colonials who settled the island. These streets radiate from a central square called *Place des Cocotiers*, named for the ancient, tall coconut palm trees which guard it. Flame Trees, ablaze this time of year with vivid scarlet blossoms, are scattered among the old statues and huge fountains found throughout the square. The old Town Hall is on one side, a thriving farmer's market just opposite. I saw a group of elderly men playing a game I remember watching in Italian neighborhoods of New York's lower east side. There it was called *boccie* but here in Nouméa it is known as *petanque*.

En Route to Espiritu Santo, November 17—Our plush, leather-seated C-87 is now only a memory. All 19 of us were unceremoniously escorted aboard a bucket-seated C-47 at dawn for the final leg of our journey to 13th Air Force Headquarters. The bumpy, noisy ride is not conducive to sleep but does not prevent me from savoring memories of *Paris-sans-Hauteur*, as Nouméa is known to some, and in particular a nightclub called "The Pacific," about which I must someday write a play. It is truly a cesspool of cast-off humanity where even those of us lucky enough to be mere observers felt fortunate to escape its confines unscathed.

* * *

Our two-hour flight to the Hebrides is due north, beginning at the southern end of New Caledonia, flying just above the spines of parallel mountain ranges which furrow the length of the island. Yawning open-pit mines, gouged from the slopes, belch clouds of dust which rise as yellow plumes. It is down there that those multi-colored, exotically costumed people of Nouméa's streets spend most of their waking hours digging out the nickle ore.

Espiritu Santo, November 17—Our approach to this beautiful island—its name, I'm told, means "Holy Ghost"—is from the south, over the town of Luganville, to an airfield called "Bomber #1." The town, as I saw it flying over, consists of a single row of one-story wooden houses strung for miles along a channel that widens to form the harbor. The waterway is now choked with rows of warships and a huge dry-dock facility.

There are five military airfields on the island, now used primarily for the movement of men and supplies to fighting fronts up north, and the return of sick and wounded to base hospitals here. I asked the driver of the truck taking us to 13th Air Force Headquarters whether the Japanese had ever bombed Espiritu Santo. "Only once," he said. "Six-eight months ago. They killed a cow."

We arrived at the beginning of the rainy season. I was convinced of that tonight, sitting through my second viewing of the movie *Watch on the Rhine* in less than a week. It was an ill-advised and poorly-timed attempt to "escape" Espiritu Santo.

The mosquitoes are pervasive; the heat is oppressive; the humidity debilitating. We are nevertheless issued two wool blankets, no sheets, with our mosquito nets.

We leave in the morning for Guadalcanal with instructions to report to 13th Air Force Bomber Command for assignment to a squadron. The inch I measured as the distance from here to there on the *Time* war map turns out to be about 600 miles.

GUADALCANAL

US Marines of the 1st Division, lining the rail of their transport ships early that Friday morning in August of 1942, were surprised to see row upon neat row of coconut palm trees extending down to the white sand of a shallow beach. The jungle they had expected was there as well, to be sure, on either side of the plantation and beyond—a sprawling, dark, green-brown, pulsating mass. Farther back, gray-brown foothills led to distant rugged black mountains. But at water's edge, the rising sun and light breezes made the palm fronds glisten and shimmer. It was the sight some Marines remembered as they climbed down to bobbing Higgins boats. The coconut palms and the jungle—and the Japanese—awaited them. The first US offensive of World War II was about to begin.

When fighting on Guadalcanal ended seven months later, in February of 1943, 1,600 Marines and Army infantrymen were dead; another 4,000 wounded. More than 60,000 US servicemen could claim a role in this watershed battle.

The Japanese knew their fate as early as December. By late January and early February, they had managed to evacuate 13,000 soldiers to Rabaul. The bodies of nearly 15,000 Japanese killed in battle were left behind in Guadalcanal's steaming jungles. Another 9,000 had died of disease. 1,000 survived as prisoners.

Unfinished Henderson Field was made ready to receive US carrier-based planes within 10 days of its capture—except when rains turned it into a quagmire. Soon, two more fighter strips were constructed, then bomber fields Carney and Koli. The "Cactus Air Force" was in business: the campaign to take back the Solomon Islands could now commence.

Guadalcanal, November 21—The Flight Engineer was our tour guide as the C-47 bringing us from Espiritu Santo approached Guadalcanal for a landing: "Florida Islands directly ahead. Tulagi where you see the docks and shacks. PT base there. Savo Island on the left, the one that looks like a volcano sticking out of the water. Our biggest naval defeat there in '42." As the plane circled back and began its descent over a coconut grove, the Engineer pointed to a stretch of shoreline off our left wing: "Red Beach. Where the Marines landed."

We were not expected by Bomber Command. Tents had to be erected. We watched and cringed as bulldozers scraped away grass and vines and black muck that looked alive with small creatures. Crushed coral soon covered over the area. Flocks of multicolored, noisy birds protested the intrusion.

I looked in vain for the legendary blue-eyed, blond nurses of movie fame. Saw only naked men with sunburned arms and necks, taking showers on outdoor raised platforms.

* * *

A much-forwarded letter from Martha Graham awaited me at Bomber Command:

> "Do not think, do!" it ordered. "So prepare yourself that you will be invincible so that you may return to fulfill your mission after this. Whatever your speech will be is not important. I know it seems to be but it is not. It is utterly important that there is a speech from you. And that is your job. So do not fail!"

Koli Point, Guadalcanal, November 25—Have moved to a tent in the 307th Group campsite at a bend of the Metapone River near Koli Point, and am assigned to the 371st Squadron—but not yet to a crew. We are within 500 yards of the runway from which I hope soon to be flying. Living conditions are much improved: this tent has a raised wooden floor, no center pole, a round table, four stools, even electric lights (three naked bulbs). Out front, there's a bonsai-size garden, sprouting a few tomato plants and several stalks of would-be sweet corn. The soil, said to be volcanic, looks black and rich. God knows, there's an abundance of rain!

The crushed-coral paths and roadways are designated "Broadway," "Fifth Avenue," and so on, by hand-lettered signs; one intersection, needless to say, is marked "Hollywood and Vine." Tents, foxholes, even bomb shelters have equally corny names: "Malaria Manor," "Fools Rush Inn," and so on, ad nauseam. It all reminds me of a Boy Scout camp I once attended at age 12.

Two of my tentmates were in the group I flew with from San Francisco, Bernard Lind and Arthur Cole. Dick Gilbert, a lanky, mustached, gravel-voiced, take-charge type came with another group. All of us bear the stigmata of "co-pilot replacement" despite our First Pilot credentials.

The food in this mess hall is no improvement over what we have been eating since leaving the States: everything is canned or dehydrated and tasteless. We spike it with three pills at each meal: vitamin, salt, and Atabrine. They do not improve the flavor. The Atabrine gives everyone a yellow complexion. Dick Gilbert says it will eventually render us impotent. Will it?

Our big concern aside from the food and not knowing whether malaria would be worse than impotency is the lack of flying time. I've not been at the controls of an airplane for more than three weeks, the longest hiatus ever. If I've forgotten how to do something, will I find out on my first combat mission?

I spend the empty hours lying on the glistening white sand of Lunga Point imagining I'm at Jones Beach on New York's Long Island, but at some remote section with palm trees and an occasional lumbering bomber or P-38 fighter skimming the blue-green waters of the bay.

The surf is familiar: small waves rolling in, unfurling like bolts of spun glass which dissolve into quivering pools of froth at my feet.

I spend guarded moments swimming to the rusting hulk of a Japanese barge mired on a sandbar, ever watchful for a prowling shark. This is a "white" beach, and shark are thought to prefer "black" sand beaches. Nevertheless I worry. I return to the beach by swimming on my back, moving my arms slowly up and down, stiffening my legs and pointing my toes, doing *battements*, and thinking of other places, other times . . .

I stop at the communal showers before returning to the tent, hang my T-shirt and shorts on the railing, stand under one of the punctured beer can nozzles. A pull of the chain releases a deluge of sun-warmed fresh water. I pull the chain a second time and close my eyes to enhance the sensation of remembered delights awakened by the water streaming down my naked body. Then I lean against the platform railing to let the sun dry my skin—and erase the memories.

Koli, Guadalcanal, November 26—The turkey was canned but I made believe it was really Thanksgiving Day, sitting there, sweltering, in a damp T-shirt and shorts, in an open-sided, thatched roof mess hall erected on an abandoned Lever Brothers coconut plantation. The table conversation was unusually desultory. I was preoccupied with thoughts of remembered faces and pleasures of another life and did not join in.

At my first-ever briefing tonight I learned, among other things, that it is a "strike," not a "mission," if bombs are dropped. It is a "sortie" if one flies into enemy territory for some other purpose—to search for a missing plane, for example, or merely to snoop around. Strikes and sorties are "counted," the total of which, plus the number of months served overseas, and hours of combat flying, give us a personal "score" used to determine when we are eligible for rest leave—or home leave.

Tomorrow at 4:30 AM the squadron will drop bombs on a small airstrip at the northern tip of Bougainville. The enemy has been observed flying in additional planes and adding anti-aircraft guns to the revetment areas. We are to discourage such efforts. I found my name on one of the crew lists designated an "Observer." A routine mission, I'm assured. Not "routine" for me: for the first time in my life, someone will be trying to kill me.

Koli, Guadalcanal, November 27—I'm to fly on Ott's plane. Never met him, nor any member of his crew. I caress the little jade goddess Martha gave me to pin on my flying suit. Once I'm aboard, Ott tells me to stay on the flight deck for the take-off. I'm to ride down below with Hill, the bombardier, the rest of the trip. The only extra oxygen hookup is in the bombardier's compartment.

I kneel behind the co-pilot's seat when we start down the runway. I see splashes of first light creep along the bottom of the eastern sky as Ott climbs the plane slowly out over the bay. He then turns us a degree or two to the left, to put us on a course over the Slot that will take us to Bougainville, three hours northwest of here.

The bombardier's compartment is a cramped, noisy, windowless space below the flight deck and directly beneath the nose gun turret. Its ceiling is too low for standing. Switches and indicator lights and instruments cover the bulkhead on the left. The bombsight fits into a floor opening at the forward end of the compartment. Hill must lie flat on his stomach to use it.

I can look down on the sea through the clear Plexiglas floor directly in front of the Sight. Hill identifies the islands as they come into view through the rising mists: Santa Isabel . . . New Georgia . . . Choiseul. . . .

We're less than half an hour out from the target. Hill reminds me it's time to put on oxygen masks. We begin circling to find our place in the formation. My feet are freezing. Now we're flying due east, towards Bougainville. I see smoke slowly rising from a mountain peak far to the south. A volcano?

The formation slowly turns as one giant plane to begin the bomb run. From my catbird seat, I look down on Buka Passage, the narrow, glistening strait of rushing water separating Bougainville from Buka island on the north. Hill tugs at my arm and points to a tiny white slash in the mottled green-black landscape: Bonis Airfield, our target.

Hill is now lying full-length, peering into the bombsight. The plane shudders as the bomb bay doors slide open. Hill turns knobs and flicks switches. I see lights flashing on a panel to his left. Then I hear him on the Intercom: "Bombs away!" I cannot see them fall. I look straight down at the Bonis runway and see a scattering of explosions. Several planes are on the tarmac, but none appear to be moving or attempting to take off. Puffs of black smoke brush the Plexiglas windscreen. I feel the plane jolt. Anti-aircraft shells are exploding all around us! Ott does not take evasive action. I hold my breath. The propellers scream as they claw at the thin air.

Then, abruptly, the formation begins to break up. Each plane is on its own, all descending swiftly towards the other side of Bougainville and down over the waters of the Pacific. Ott aims us directly at the white-hot mirror of the rising sun. When we are only a few hundred feet from the ocean, he levels us off, then reverses direction in a great sweeping turn, holding the left wing nearly vertical. We head back towards Bougainville only slightly above the cresting waves.

The instructions given at last night's briefing called for us to return from Bonis along Bougainville's eastern coast, to fly single file at treetop height, and to shoot up all native structures we see; but no natives, no animals. We are meant to show the natives that allied forces, not Japanese, are still the boss on Bougainville.

We head south, following the palm-shaded strip of white sand, flying so low I can easily see the gunners' 50mm tracer shells streaming into the little leaf huts, setting fire to the thatched roofs, kicking dust after fleeing pigs.

I stare straight down through the Plexiglas floor and watch small naked black men stiffly standing, legs apart, shaking their fists up at us. One of the warriors lofts his spear. Another throws a stone.

Koli, Guadalcanal, November 29—Long talk tonight with Dick Gilbert, most senior among the four of us sharing this tent, certainly wisest in the ways of the military, and unique in having piloted an airplane before joining the Air Force. More intriguing still, to my mind, is learning that this lanky, unsmiling, mustached former airplane mechanic is, in fact, a musician at heart, a jazz pianist by night, and one-time accompanist of silent films at old-time movie houses in San Francisco.

Dick is astonishingly like Ralph G., Martha's rehearsal and class accompanist: same deep, raspy voice; small dark sunken eyes; hollow cheeks; lantern jaw. Cigarette always dangling from the corner of the mouth.

Even their music resumés are similar: Ralph also improvised accompaniments for silent films and played piano at jazz bars, but his legacy was the Cornish School in Seattle, where he began a career playing for dance classes. It was at the Martha Graham Dance Studio, on lower Fifth Avenue in New York, where I got to know Ralph—and Merce Cunningham, one among several dancers who came from the Cornish School:

It is 4:30 on the afternoon of a late October day in 1941, and I am sitting on the cold linoleum Studio floor, at the back of the room, screened from Martha's eyes—I hope—by the other members of the class, all more technically proficient than I. We await the arrival of Ralph, the accompanist, hoping Martha will not lose patience and begin without him. It feels more like a performance than a class with Ralph's music.

At 4:32, Ralph sidles into the hushed room, sits immediately at the battered old grand and raises his hands high above the keyboard. A few of us dare to applaud. Ralph's tentative smile instantly dissolves with Martha's flung command: "Bounces!" We poise ourselves as if preparing for a levitational flight: back stiffened and straight to the top of the head; soles of the feet pressed together and pulled back to our crotch; heels off the floor; knees and thighs lifted; arms to the side; hands on the floor. ("The tension in one's body must give the impression of a vibration.")

". . . And!" Martha warns, turning to Ralph. His hands crash down on the keys. A shattering, dissonant chord propels our first "bounce." The chord is repeated and we attempt to "bounce" our rigid torsos forward and back, forward and back. The beat is just a bit faster than we can "bounce," the chord now pianissimo and staccato. A slight melody soon becomes apparent and is repeated, slightly altered, as we extend our legs forward on Martha's cue, lean over our knees, still "bouncing," and touching our toes with the heels of our hands. The melody Ralph has devised becomes today's theme, and the variations accompany our movements for the next 90 minutes.

Without prompting, the class as one begins the next in Martha's litany of Floor Exercises: Sit to the Side; Exercise on Six; the Pleadings. Ralph's strident, insistent music masks my groans. Martha walks among us, correcting arm positions, leg angles, hip turn-out, sometimes with flick of her fingers; or in a stage whisper everyone is meant to hear. She exhorts us to push harder, reach farther, bend deeper, turn faster.

When we finally rise from the floor, I feel I am standing erect for the first time in my life. The wall of mirrors we now face magnifies all my errors, reveals my physical inadequacies. We begin the brushes, sliding the bare foot forward, without bending the knee, until it is just off the floor; then to the sides. The rustle and scraping of the feet is the only sound we hear until Ralph adds off-beat staccato chords to keep the tempo steady.

We assume Second Position. Martha calls it the "Battle position of the world." She once told us that the Indian dancer, Uday Shan-Kar, is a Warrior when in Second Position Plié with the whole foot flat on the ground; that when he lifts just his big toe, he is a Hero.

Ralph smooths our Deep Pliés with pedaled glissandos. Then come the Extensions and Turns, followed by Sits and Slow Falls. ("A Sit or a Fall does not finish on the floor. The floor is only the means by which one rises.") As we Jump-in-Place, Martha warns: "The beat is UP! Pay attention to Ralph's silences!"

An hour has passed. We are now gathered in a far corner of the studio, ready to begin the Floor Crossings. Ralph lights another cigarette and plays a little circus fanfare as we Prance-in-Place to loosen our leg muscles. The girls always lead this procession. It begins with Low Walks, back leg dragging, knees bent, arms swinging. We strain to keep on the beat, which Ralph speeds up and syncopates. Triplets next: a Demi-Plié followed by two level steps, accent on the Plié—like a waltz, which Ralph simulates by plucking notes from the upper register.

The exultation of running makes everyone smile, even Martha. ("The dancer must sparkle, as a spontaneous laugh.") She is now standing near the piano, calling attention to each unpointed foot, bent knee, open mouth, limp wrist. We run as fast as we dare, first high and erect, then low in a squat, next on tip-toe. Finally, we skip. Small Leaps follow, then Run-Skip-Leaps. The finale is always of Great Leaps: Up! and-Up! and-Up! Ralph accents the second of each four beats with a staccato chord.

The last to cross is usually Merce, who does the Great Leaps with left arm extended, right forearm raised. He seems to briefly float in mid-air. As he lands at the far end of the studio, Ralph concludes the final variation of today's musical theme with a cascade of descending arpeggios. We face Martha and applaud. She smiles, genuflects to Ralph. He grins and drags deeply on the stub of his smoldering cigarette.

Koli, Guadalcanal, December 1—I am still without a crew assignment and today suffered guilt pangs for this otherwise somewhat fortunate—if boring—status. As I knew it would inevitably happen, one of the squadron's planes failed to return from today's strike. Kahili was the target. They said at de-briefing that it was Gwicky's crew that got it. Hit full-on by a Zeke as they left the bomb run. Their plane, the "Mary-Jane," exploded and burned all the way down. No 'chutes. Hit the water close to Poporang; cartwheeled and sank. No rafts. The Zeke strafed the oil-slick.

The Major came by late this afternoon looking for Gwicky's tent. Dick pointed to it, across the street from ours. Then I knew who Gwicky was. All the racket that kept us awake last night came from that tent. Singing . . . yelling . . . carrying on. Everyone in the area told them to knock it off. Did no good. I finally fell asleep. Seemed minutes later when the wake-up whistle was being blown in my ear. I had no mission to get up for, counted my blessings, and watched the other guys slouch off in the darkness. Including Gwicky and his loudmouth tentmates.

The Major spent a half-hour or so in Gwicky's tent. Said he would send someone from S-2 to inventory the guys' stuff and decide what to send back to the families. The Major said it was their fourth mission, adding: "The first five are the hardest."

I'm two down, three to go.

Koli, Guadalcanal, December 3—I have been assigned to Midthun's crew, moved into their tent and today flew my first combat mission as a co-pilot. The men are all "old-timers" out here, very professional and skilled in handling their jobs. At least it seems so on the basis of one mission.

Our plane is one I've already heard of, the legendary "Frenisi," whose name comes from an Artie Shaw hit tune, "Frenesi," but misspelled when painted on the nose of the plane. Anyway, "Frenisi" has the most missions flown to date of any 13th Air Force B-24. I counted 47 of the little bomb symbols painted on its nose. A life-size portrait of Miss "Frenisi" is painted on the fuselage under my co-pilot's window.

Today's mission was to Bonis, where I went on my very first strike. Anti-aircraft fire was heavy and "Frenisi's" tail took some flak. I was unaware of the hit and no one mentioned it until we returned to Koli. Our flight engineer, a profane but mechanical genius from Texas, called Scotty, said the damage was minor. "Fuckin' Japs can't even hit a B-24 straight on," was his assessment, and declared the mission a "milk-run" and a waste of time.

Not a waste of time for me. I quickly learned how different it is to fly co-pilot on a combat equipped, armor-plated B-24 from the stripped-down training planes I flew out of Maxwell Field. I had great difficulty holding "Frenisi" in place in formation at altitude. She "mushed" and drifted and skidded, seemed underpowered, unresponsive and, sometimes, completely unmaneuverable. Of course, the thin air at 20-thousand feet, and the extra weight of a fully-loaded plane, added to my woes.

Midthun was well aware of my inexperience as a combat co-pilot and I got a full quota of prompting stares. He's long since forgotten his days as a co-pilot, now gives the impression he can fly the plane all by himself. Seems irritated that some of the knobs and levers and switches and pedals were placed on the co-pilot's side of the plane, out of his reach.

On the basis of this one mission, I've decided he's a deadly serious, humorless "old" man; a good pilot but not a "flyer."

Jeff Peterson, the navigator, called "Pete" by the crew, is casual to a fault about this combat business. I find his attitude somewhat off-putting. Pete is considered one of Group's top navigators, but, like Midthun, he does not seem to "enjoy" flying.

"Frenisi's" bombardier, Rumsey, is difficult to peg. He talks very little, never about combat or flying or his home, wherever that is. His conversation consists mostly of "yes's" and "no's."

* * *

The first letter addressed to the Guadalcanal APO number is from Martha and was written Thanksgiving Day:

> "Your life must now take on the quality of a performance. I can imagine the magnification of all sensations."

Koli, Guadalcanal, December 5—The target this morning was a place called Tsirogei, four hours up The Slot, off the northwest coast of Bougainville. It's a Jap barge repair facility. We'd been in the air only a couple of hours— it was not yet 7:00—when Midthun told me to check the aileron controls; said they felt sluggish to him. I turned the wheel back and forth several times. Ailerons seemed O.K. to me, I told Midthun. Not O.K., said Midthun, and ordered Rumsey to salvo the bombs. Then Midthun turned us around and told Pete to give him a course home.

Pete took us back down The Slot close to the east coast of New Georgia. He pointed out a string of tiny, tree-covered islands in a lagoon that followed the entire length of the island. Pete said it formed the largest lagoon of its kind in the world: Morovo Lagoon.

* * *

Short letter today from Merce in New York alluding to my possible fate out here. I was genuinely moved—and surprised—by his bringing up the subject. Does he know, as I do, how futile are attempts to evade one's fate? MG wrote recently that I have only to remain spiritually strong to preserve the "flame" that will "temper" me to the moment. Amen.

* * *

Patlock, our ground crew chief, could find nothing wrong with "Frenisi's" ailerons.

Koli, Guadalcanal, December 7—Most second anniversaries are easily ignored, and today's is, somewhat surprisingly, no exception even though all of us on this island of regret are here because of what happened to Pearl two years ago, and should at least acknowledge the fact.

> *It is December 7, 1941, and I am on a train slowly tracing the outer fringes of the Okefenokee, pressing my face to a window, futilely searching for alligators. We have come all the way from Rome, Georgia, this morning, and hope to be in Miami by midafternoon. There, the fifteen of us traveling together, the Martha Graham Dance Company, will board a ship for Havana.*
>
> *Now a conductor enters our coach to announce that the next stop will be Jacksonville. He proceeds up the aisle, stopping frequently to talk to passengers. When he approaches our group, he motions us to gather in. I hear only words: ". . . Pearl Harbor bombed . . . Japanese planes . . . early this morning . . ." Jean Erdman, seated across the aisle from me, stifles a cry. David Campbell tells the conductor his parents, too, live in Honolulu. When the train stops in Jacksonville, the conductor directs them to a telephone, but all circuits to Honolulu are busy.*
>
> *In Miami, we learn the ship's departure for Havana has been delayed until after dark. Sitting in a restaurant, waiting, we hear FDR on the radio declaring war. Jean and David at last get through to Honolulu: their families are unharmed and safe. For now.*
>
> *We stay at the palatial Hotel Nacional de Cuba on the Malecon. The spacious room I share with Sascha Liebich has floor-to-ceiling casement windows, marble floors, a louvered door to the hallway. There are six towels, in graduated sizes, for each of us, hanging on heated pipes in the bathroom. Downstairs, I see patched bullet holes in corridor walls. "Batista's fingerprints," a porter whispers.*
>
> *We give our two scheduled performances before returning to Miami on the last ship permitted to make this roundtrip voyage. Merce did not dance with us. He was forbidden to leave the U.S. by his draft board. I failed the audition to replace him in El Penitente. It was then that I knew I was not really a dancer and never would be one.*

That is what I remember today, on the second anniversary of Pearl Harbor Day.

Koli, Guadalcanal, December 10—Will I ever see Tsirogei? For the second time this week, "Frenisi" failed to reach it. Again, we were only about two hours out from Koli when Midthun decided to abort the mission. This time he claimed there was a "flutter" in the rudder. Last time it was a "sluggish" aileron. Patlock, the crew chief, found nothing wrong with the ailerons then; he won't find a "flutter" in the rudder this time. But Midthun will not be persuaded.

He was in a heavy sweat when he discovered the "problem" this morning: ripped off those skin-tight leather dress gloves he always wears. "Take over!" he shouted at me. I did. "See?" he challenged. "Feel the flutter?" I didn't. Felt guilty and disloyal. Did not feel a flutter in the rudder.

* * *

Told Pete today about flying out here in Eleanor Roosevelt's plane, the C-87 she used on her inspection trip to Australia. He smiled. Remembered her stop-over here on the 'Canal on the return flight. Said he caught a glimpse of her at the movie that night. Only a glimpse because the movie was interrupted by a fake Red Alert. Staged for her benefit. Everyone mad as hell when the projector was shut off. Pete said the next morning a cartoon appeared on the Squadron bulletin board. It showed a recognizable Eleanor lifting her skirt to a pipe in the ground with funnel stuck in the top, one of those ubiquitous "Pee Tubes" that make the area smell so profoundly of urine. The cartoon caption read: "How do you navigate this thing?"

Koli, Guadalcanal, December 12—I assiduously perform little acts of formality on the eve of missions. Martha says this will prevent the creatures from breaking through. I always re-pin the tiny jade goddess to the lapel of my flying suit; and transfer to another pocket the miniature copy of the *Bhagavad-Gita* she loaned to me which I always carry—but seldom read; lay out my cleanest pair of khakis and a shirt with epaulets. I then oil and reload the .45 with tracer shells, so the gun could be used for signaling as well as killing; and strop the blade of the hunting knife: it must be sharp enough to slit a man's throat or gut a wild pig. Finally, I write a letter. I always think of it as a "last" letter, no matter to whom it is addressed.

I check the mission loading lists, posted on the Group bulletin board, before going to the mess hall. My name leaps out at me: "1st Lt. Zellmer, D. E., Co-Pilot." I draw a circled "Z" beside the name, as I began doing in college, on lecture attendance lists.

We four tentmates always sit together at this meal. Pete says a little extra "bonding" can't hurt. But we never talk about the upcoming mission, only about "home," what we did before the war, what we have learned in letters from home.

The Briefing always seem unnecessarily perfunctory to me considering that some 240 lives will be at risk on the mission. So much is taken for granted. It is always assumed we will be "lucky," never "surprised" and inevitably "successful." Even Pete, who has 35 missions to my five, is optimistic about tomorrow's strike on Ballale. I am somewhat unsettled on hearing the Major casually note that the airstrip we will bomb was constructed by 500 British POWs the Japs imported from Singapore. He said that the few British still alive when the runway was completed were executed.

I nod to someone I recognize, someone I never see at the mess hall or at the Club. Only at briefings. And have never talked with. Would I remember him if he were dangling from a parachute? Or peering out the hatch of a burning plane?

It's still dark when we finish breakfast. Scrambled powdered eggs and Spam. A snarling pack of 6 × 6 trucks is waiting outside to take us to the airfield. Their spluttering, backfiring engines dissemble the pre-dawn stillness.

I sit as far forward as possible in the truck's cargo bed, hoping to avoid the exhaust fumes rising in our wake. We follow a narrow, crushed-coral road winding through the jungle. I lean outward to bathe my face in the cooling night air. From time to time we pass through an unseen cloud of a strange, exotic scent rising from *fleurs du mal* on the jungle floor.

"Frenisi" awaits us in the shadows of her hardstand, a giant pre-historic bird now betrayed by the half-light of dawn. Her wing-tip lights slowly blink on and off, on and off. I watch Tex, our flight engineer, on his knees peering underneath "Frenisi." Is he confirming her sex?

We are now at the head of the runway. I hold the brake pedals down with both feet; Midthun pushes each throttle forward, one by one, until its engine screams in protest. When the tower finally flashes the green light, I release the brakes. "Frenisi" charges forward. As we hurtle past the tower, an outstretched arm waves us into the sky. "Frenisi" slowly lifts off the tarmac and begins the climb into the first light of the day.

"Keep her at 310-degrees," orders Pete. We do. That's where Ballale is.

Koli, Guadalcanal, December 17—Yesterday's strike at Bonis, only my sixth, will be my last for at least six weeks. Current policy calls for air crew personnel to go on rest leave after six weeks of combat flying. By my calculations, I have been in the South Pacific for only four weeks—but my name is on the list.

We continue flying during this period but do only test-hops, training flights, and so on. Sometime during the six weeks we are supposed to have a week's leave in Auckland, New Zealand. Since getting there involves a 2,000-mile flight each way, availability of transport planes is the critical factor. I will keep my fingers permanently crossed.

The Bonis strike was meant to destroy revetment areas only. We had been assured the runway was already out of commission, and aerial photos they showed us proved it: the strip was pock-marked with bomb craters from one end to the other. And so it looked when we began the bomb run. Unfortunately, just then we saw three Jap fighters taking off from the supposedly bombed-out runway. The fighters were either Zekes or Hamps—I couldn't tell which—and the first Jap planes I have seen. They had the turned-down wing tips and raised canopy of the plane everyone calls a "Zero." But they did not attack us—merely hung off to the side as we proceeded to make the bomb run. An audacious gesture, I thought. But of course there were only three of them and twelve of us, and each of our B-24s was armed with ten .50 caliber machineguns. I suspect the fighters were up there merely to give their ground gun crews our course and altitude. Regardless, none of our planes were hit, and the Jap fighters landed back on that presumably bombed-out runway.

S-2 had no explanation of how Jap planes could take off and land on a runway filled with bomb craters.

Koli, Guadalcanal, December 20—A letter today from Martha responding to my account of the first combat mission I flew. "Perhaps," she writes, "it brings some of the strange beauty of awareness that participating in a great tragic play gives."

Martha said the Company is rehearsing *Punch*, adding: "You are constantly in our efforts to remember 'what David did.' Kinch knows he has your role on a loan. . . . Your other self walks about with us daily."

My Guadalcanal "self" feels that other life slowly slipping from my grasp. I cling to the dimming memories in a desperate effort to insure my return to that world.

* * *

Got the explanation today of how those three Jap fighters were able to fly off that bombed out runway at Bonis. The runway had been hit by our bombs, but the craters were filled in with coral and gravel, then soaked with oil, which made them appear black, like craters, in the aerial photographs.

Koli, Guadalcanal, December 23—It's only 10:00 AM but I'm already taking occasional sips from our communal bottle of "mission" whiskey. We're entitled to an ounce of "medicinal rye" after each mission. The four of us collect our shares weekly from the Flight Surgeon, and save it for special occasions in this one bottle.

I've decided these last few days before Christmas are a "special occasion." I sit here fighting back the same old ghosts that appear from time to time, wondering what it will take to make me whole again.

* * *

On days like today, when our crew is not scheduled for a mission, we officers spend an hour or two reading enlisted men's outgoing mail, making sure no war secrets or invasion plans are being leaked to mothers and girlfriends. One letter that got passed to me was written by someone who, unbelievably, is happy and content with this life out here. He writes of frequent visits to native villages—which I thought were off-limits—to attend religious ceremonies and so on. I gather he knows the language, is apparently friendly with a local chief, and rather eloquently proclaims his admiration for the natives' simple, unaffected life.

I noted that the letter was written to a minister friend and that the GI is a clerk at Bomber Command headquarters. He's not in harm's way there.

Koli, Guadalcanal, December 24—Pete and I acquired a jeep today and drove to Lunga Beach. Strange that swimming always seems worth the risk of tangling with a shark; we're constantly warned of the possibility.

The surf was shark-free, and after an hour or so making believe we were at Waikiki, we lay on the sand and tried to forget where we really were; and talked about the world we didn't quite make before coming out here.

Later, as we walked back to the Jeep, I saw Sam, by himself, coming towards us. Sam and I have known one another since our early days in flight training—more than a year; and we almost became close friends during those last joyous, frantic days just before coming here. We haven't seen one another since arriving a month ago.

Our paths on the beach were some distance apart. I waved, shouted "Hi!" Sam waved, smiled, and shouted "Hi!" Neither of us stopped. Why?

Koli, Guadalcanal, December 26—Christmas Eve, as I feared, was excessively celebrated. The Officers Club, because of the occasion, dispensed drinks from the bar's own supply, not from our private bottles of hoarded "mission" whiskey. Rum eventually replaced the 25¢ bourbon and rye, and one soon forgot that buying a round for "the house" meant buying 80 drinks.

I remember few details but knew from my aches and pains the next day that I must have demonstrated Graham "sits," as I am wont to do if encouraged. In this maneuver, one stands with feet wide apart and turned "out," then literally sits down between the legs by twisting the upper body to the right or left, all the while holding the back very straight. One ends up sitting, knees crossed, facing to the rear. One untwists the body while rising to resume the original position—not a simple task while wearing "GI" boots!

I do remember "dueling" with someone, but not why; presenting him with my "card," a gum wrapper. We stood back-to-back for a moment, then withdrew the obligatory five paces, turned, and proceeded to throw our drinks of rum into one another's face.

There was canned turkey for Christmas dinner, some cards and letters to re-read, and two books from Martha, mailed on December 10th: St. Exupery's *The Little Prince* and T. S. Eliot's *Collected Poems*.

* * *

Read in an old Minneapolis newspaper at the Club today that Leonard Bernstein was named assistant conductor of the New York Philharmonic and has already substituted for Bruno Walter on one occasion. Could this be the "Lennie" I once heard give an impromptu, mock performance of *Tristan und Isolde*, singing all the roles, male and female?

It was a Saturday afternoon in early October of 1942, remembered because it was my last weekend in New York before reporting to the Air Force. I had given up my Charles Street room and was spending these few remaining days of freedom, rent free, at the apartment David Campbell and Ethel Butler had fashioned in the space of a defunct street-level restaurant, *The Rendezvous*, on East 13th Street, just off Fifth Avenue. I slept on a cot in the narrow entrance hall between the Mens and Ladies bathrooms.

The large, street-facing dining room now held David and Ethel's bed, a chair and lamp or two, and David's old, battered upright—always well-tuned—on which he pursued his project of transcribing the major musical themes of Stravinsky's *Le Sacre du printemps* into separate colors which he carefully traced in crayon above the musical notes on specially designed score sheets.

On this particular Saturday afternoon, David and Ethel had invited a few of our mutual friends to a very informal farewell party, but Lennie Bernstein, whom David knew, just happened to stop by, a tall, statuesque brunette in tow, whom he introduced as his "copyist." I later learned she was a semi-professional model, trying to escape the attentions of a sculptress with whom she formerly lived by moving in with Lennie and pretending to be his girlfriend.

Bernstein was familiar with David's Stravinsky project, and the two spent some time at the piano discussing it while the rest of us drank Ethel's Fish House Punch. Before many drinks, we heard Stravinsky's dissonances replaced by Wagner's endless melodies and Lennie was launched on his abbreviated version of *Tristan*, which, accelerated by Ethel's punch, made that afternoon a memorable occasion. But I would not have guessed, then, that Lennie Bernstein would end up in Carnegie Hall. I'd have guessed it might be a very different kind of music hall, perhaps one more likely frequented by Noel Coward than Bruno Walter.

1944

Koli, Guadalcanal, January 3—It is now official that I will go to Auckland for a week. I do not know the date of departure but I will be sustained during my wait by dreams of sleeping between clean, white sheets—alone or otherwise—with the scent of perfume on my pillow and the taste of lipstick on my mouth. I dream excessively of shaves and shampoos and massages and scalding hot showers. And girls.

* * *

Cultural news from all over, as reported on the Group bulletin board today:

"Betty Grable is the number one box office attraction. Bob Hope is second."

Watch on the Rhine was voted best film of 1943 by the New York Film Critics.

Variety reports the most popular songs are (1) "Shoo Shoo Baby," (2) "People Will Say We Are In Love," and (3) "Oh, What A Beautiful Morning."

Judged the outstanding books of 1943 by "Book-of-the-Month Club" were John P. Marquand's *So Little Time* and Wendell Willkie's *One World*.

Koli, Guadalcanal, January 6—Still awaiting word on when I will leave for Auckland. Pass the time reading, writing letters, and exploring the paths that skirt the jungle. Have found trees bearing bananas, papaya, coconuts, of course; orchids and hibiscus flourish here. Screeching cockatoos are everywhere. White parrots flutter about like giant moths. The line of mountains one sees on the horizon suggest the Rockies from this distance; but the jungle sounds and sights, and head-high, razor-sharp kunai grass assure me I am still on Guadalcanal.

* * *

Franny Benn Hall writes that she will send me books, if I like, from the bookstore in Westwood Village where she works part-time. It is near the UCLA campus where she and her husband are grad students. I could purchase the books at her discount rate. The postscript to her letter triggered a flood of memories: "What if we *had* gone to Elsinore?"

> *It's a sunny, warming, early October morning in 1938 and I am walking down Bascom Hill on the University of Wisconsin's Madison campus. I have just come from a Sociology lecture, and the strident rantings of Adolph Hitler still echo in my head. The entire hour was spent listening to recordings of broadcasts by the Fuhrer. His is not the language of Goethe or Schiller that I am struggling to master in my German class. Coming from his mouth, the language is a weapon for screaming and shouting; a rapier one minute, a club the next.*
>
> *I am on my way to the Student Union to meet Franny. I hesitate at the corner of the Library to see if the ROTC recruits are drilling. They are. I hope they will still be there for our noon-time anti-ROTC rally.*
>
> *I find Franny already on the terrace. We watch the few lonely sailboats still braving Mendota's whipped, opaque waters while I tell her about the Hitler speeches. Then she tells me her exciting news: A small, work-cooperative college in Denmark is offering scholarships to American college students. Two spaces have been reserved for Wisconsin. The school is located in Elsinore—Hamlet's Elsinore! If selected, one would need only enough money for freighter passage and personal expenses. We decide to apply immediately.*

* * *

> *Our applications were approved before Christmas, subject to the status of the war next fall. We made what plans we could and followed the progress of the*

war with fingers crossed. Then, on April 9, Denmark surrendered to the Germans.

The next day, we met again on the Student Union terrace. Mendota was still winter-frozen and iceboats now sailed on its glinting surface. The terrace was wind-swept and deserted. We talked briefly of what might have been, then parted. As I walked back to my room on State Street, I passed the drill field by the Library where ROTC recruits still marched, now in even greater numbers.

En Route to Auckland, January 11—Four hours from now I'll be back in the 20th century, and re-enter the world of automobiles, paved streets, tall buildings, restaurants—and pretty girls.

Our C-87 is high above the Coral Sea. Moments ago we passed over tiny Norfolk Island, the only bit of land in the 900-mile stretch of water between New Caledonia and New Zealand. Ben, my seatmate, says descendants of *Bounty* mutineers live there.

Ben's an Intelligence Officer at Group Headquarters. He sometimes de-briefs our flight crews. We came to know one another soon after I joined the squadron, back in November, when I asked him for some research material on the Solomon Islands. Any particular island, he wondered? Choiseul, I suggested, liking the sound of the word. No paper on Choiseul, he said, but he could recommend a good hotel in Paris by that name: *Hotel de France et Choiseul*, on the Place Vendôme. "The family always stays there," he said.

Ben's on Rest Leave, too. Now he wants to talk about the last three days we spent at Espiritu Santo. He marvels still at my luck in finding Frankie there, a Navy nurse I met in San Francisco on my last night before coming overseas. She was with a group of other Navy nurses at the "Top of the Mark," celebrating their last night before departing by ship for the South Pacific. We talked long enough to decide we wanted to stay in touch, and exchanged APO addresses. Eventually a letter from her reached me on Guadalcanal. Her return address, I knew from the code, was Espiritu Santo, which she was forbidden to name in the letter.

Our brief stay on "Buttons," Espiritu Santo's code name, was spent exclusively with the Navy, Frankie's Navy. I had only to locate the Base Hospital to find her. She and her friend, Janie, in their crisp, white uniforms, unashamedly escorted the two of us, in our wrinkled khakis, G.I. boots, and skin-head haircuts, to a Navy's Officers Club that even offered ice cold milk, a Mess Hall with cloth-covered tables, napkins, and white-coated waiters, and to the movies where we sat on folding chairs—not log benches—under a canvas roof. We almost regretted having to leave Espiritu Santo. Almost.

I was happy to see Frankie, of course, and Ben was delighted to have lucked into a "blind" double date as pretty as Ginny. But Espiritu Santo, Navy nurses notwithstanding, still had mosquitos and jungles and humidity and constant rain. We wanted what Auckland promised: civilization!

The girls presented us with a bottle of vitamin pills as a farewell present. We were instructed to take one with each meal, two before drinks at our favorite pub.

*   *   *

Auckland, January 13—My hotel is just off Queen Street, Auckland's main thoroughfare, and a trolley clangs by the front entrance throughout the day. There is a sink with running water in my room, and clean white sheets on the bed. Can this be paradise?

My arrival the day before yesterday did not begin with much promise. The roommate I drew was a co-pilot named Shedd: large, slow-moving, abnormally small eyes, a thin, colorless mustache on his upper lip, and wearing wrinkled, soiled khakis. On the short walk to the building where we were to get the obligatory physical examination, I learned he came from some place in Tennessee. Half an hour into the examination, I learned, from one of the corpsmen, that Shedd's entire body was covered with lice, and he was being sprayed with DDT in an unused shower stall.

The flight surgeon found me a bit underweight but otherwise fit enough for a week in Auckland. I proceeded (without Shedd) to the floor below to pick up my ration of liquor: one bottle of Scotch, with which I had also to buy one each of gin and sherry to help perpetuate the myth that servicemen will drink anything. Ben was there, too, and we decided to find a pub and sample the local brew.

Some hours later, after quickly learning that one must double-pay the barmaid for each beer to insure continuing rounds before the supply ran out, and then being directed to a nearby restaurant that featured fresh oysters as well as steak-and-eggs, we returned to the hotel.

We smelled smoke as soon as we reached my floor, and then saw it curling out from under the door to my room. Inside, we found Shedd passed-out-drunk, sitting on the floor, leaning back against his bed. A large section of the top blanket was smoldering, in the center of which we found a burning cigarette. We pulled Shedd away from the bed, doused the blanket with water, then called the front desk for fresh bed clothes.

After reviving Shedd, somewhat, and determining he had suffered no burns, we got him back on the newly made bed, confiscated all his liquor and cigarettes, and departed.

Ben said there was a spare bed in his room so I collected my still-unpacked B-4 bag and followed him down the hall.

Auckland, January 16—Everyone in Auckland, including the New Zealanders, is having such a good time, one forgets, from time to time, that New Guinea and Guadalcanal still lurk out there, just beyond the horizon. Even more disturbing, I never think about New York.

*   *   *

The following observations after only five days in this Kiwi heaven: The British-sounding accent makes everyone seem well-educated and cultured. An unfounded assumption, I learned, when dating a girl by phone. . . . The climate is like Florida's, with the seasons reversed, but the countryside looks more like California. . . . Everyone carries a book or magazine or newspaper. There are bookstores and newsstands on virtually every corner. And judging by overheard tram conversations, even day-laborers are well-informed. . . . As a large city, Auckland is not sophisticated or modern as, say, New York or San Francisco, but gives the impression it wants to be considered as such. The real attraction, for me, is its old world charm: the tiny European cars, the dilapidated trams, the old-fashioned chemist shops, the neat, prim churches, the luxuriant city gardens and parks at every turn. I even enjoy struggling with the monetary system, trying to figure out the pence, shillings, florins, crowns. But what is a "guinea?"

To survive, however, one must quickly adjust to the left-hand traffic system. Bicycles are the greatest threat. Watching the right-hand drive Austins race through the vortex of a rotary makes me dizzy. I must stand very still, shut my eyes, and figure the whole thing out before stepping off the curb.

Auckland, January 18—A large crowd gathering on the Quay at noontime today distracted Ben and me from our search for a new restaurant. A parade seemed to be in progress, complete with drums and trumpets. We hurried down Queen Street to see what it was all about. And quickly learned it was a demonstration to protest the presence of "the bloody Yanks" while New Zealand soldiers remained in the jungles and deserts abroad. Ben and I headed back down Queen Street as quickly as possible.

We had just come from a visit to a favorite hotel bar's daily 11:30 "Pub Crawl" for several glasses of New Zealand's famous strong, bitter—if warm—beer. As is true at the "Five O'Clock Swill," also for men only, the beer supply lasts less than an hour, after which an even more limited supply of Scotch is available at 12¢ per glass. The very thirsty can then resort to gin of various colors and liqueurs in assorted flavors until "Time, Gentlemen!" is called.

* * *

Tonight, word has it, "everyone" is going to the largest night club in town, a movie theatre about the size of the Paramount in New York City, that opens as a night club at 10:30, after the movie. The orchestra seats are removed to make room for a dance floor, a large band, and tables for the patrons.

All movie theatres in Auckland are very elaborate affairs, and have the same status as a Broadway legitimate theatre. All seats for the movies are reserved, and one can be seated only at the beginning of the one performance given each night. Unfortunately, the movies shown are the same tired, old Hollywood fare we watch in our outdoor jungle theatres. Here in Auckland we visit these lavish palaces only if our date insists.

Last night, the night club of choice was the "Trocadero," and as usual, we almost literally "bought" the orchestra and dictated what songs it would play. We always outnumber the New Zealanders at these clubs. We closed the "Trocadero" at dawn this morning, long after all New Zealanders—except for our dates—had left. Is it any wonder they hold rallies to protest our presence?

Koli, Guadalcanal, January 30—I had to endure six rainy, sweltering days on Espiritu Santo awaiting transportation back to this even more unforgiving island. My head remained full of Auckland dreams even as my heart led me to think only of Frankie. I once again succumbed to the romance of the situation, but whereas I was rendered speechless the last time we were together, on this occasion I succumbed to the first pale yellow moon we watched lift from the sea and said things I could not truly mean even in that scenario. I must now attempt to exorcise those words from both our memories.

On the last day, Ben and I visited a small aircraft carrier tied up in Segond Channel, just off Luganville. We were made very welcome aboard and invited to stay for lunch. I found myself sitting opposite someone I quickly recognized as Roland Ball, at whose Cornell University fraternity house we men from the Graham Dance Company once stayed after giving a concert on campus. A year or so later, Ball was in New York and visited Merce and me at our West 12th Street apartment. He was by then on the faculty at Cornell; he's now a Radar Officer in the US Navy.

Read this announcement on the ship's Bulletin Board:

U.S. FORCES TODAY LANDED ON KWAJALEIN AND MAJURO ATOLLS IN MARSHALL ISLANDS.

Koli, Guadalcanal, February 1—Nearly two weeks have passed since I sighed a reluctant farewell to Auckland, and my days and nights are still haunted by disparate memories of that Kiwi paradise: pretty young girls caroling "Hi, Yank! Watch it!" whenever we stepped into the wrong traffic lane; platters of raw oysters and thick steaks topped with eggs; pitchers of ice cold sweet milk or warm, bitter beer; hot showers whenever, and cool, clean sheets to dream on . . .

I especially remember the afternoons at the darkened "Jewel Box" night-club owned by an attractive Hungarian refugee "of a certain age," where I was free to use the house piano to attempt "Clair de Lune" and one-finger "Zing! Went The Strings of My Heart" for Dick Gilbert, hoping he would teach it to the house band. ("Frenesi" had already been added to its repertoire.)

"The Countess," as the club owner was known, sometimes invited Dick and me to her private table just at closing time to share a Scotch as she reminisced about the Budapest to which she longed to return. . . .

Koli, Guadalcanal, February 4—Rest leave continues and I remain exempt from combat missions flown daily and almost exclusively on targets in the Rabaul area. I take as many test flights as are offered but I am mostly on the ground, astride my newly white-sheeted cot, courtesy the US Navy hospital on Espiritu Santo, re-reading the many letters that arrived while I was away.

The letter I have no need to re-read, as I know it almost from memory by now, is Martha's telling of the December 26th premier New York performance of her *Deaths and Entrances* and the still untitled solo based on Elinor Wylie's poems. The house was sold-out, the critics wrote good notices, even though some found *Deaths* obscure. The audience seemed "baffled but moved," Martha said. Someone forgot to turn on the off-stage microphone so Merce could be heard reading the Wylie poems while Martha danced the solo, but the evening was so well received, the entire program was scheduled to be repeated two weeks later, a tribute to Martha's unlikely and unexplained popularity.

The most personally moving paragraph in the letter is the first, relating that as she was standing alone on the stage, just before the curtain, she looked up into the flies and spoke my name.

In another part of the letter she astonishes me by praising my letters to her, saying they are quite "rare," that she has kept them all, and thinks they could be edited and used in some way. She goes on to make an even more startling suggestion, that I might consider writing something for her! She said she wants to do a dance piece with Samuel Barber on a theme of "a man speaking to a woman across distance," a kind of soliloquy on various subjects, possibly a flyer's thoughts while in combat. "Perhaps you can write your deaths and entrances in such ways that endear life for others," she concludes.

To date, Martha's challenging proposal has produced only sleepless nights.

Koli, Guadalcanal, February 12—Ben says S-2 is of the opinion that all Japanese warships have left Rabaul and been relocated in the Palaus, not Truk. This suggests a major shift in Japanese naval strategy, and could mean the end of aggressive naval action by the enemy in the Solomons.

Ben does not tell me everything he knows. Only what I "need" to know, he explains. He has told me a little about his personal life. Again, what I "need" to know, I suppose. Home is in Purchase, N.Y. The house has a name: "Seeaway." His father is in banking, a career Ben expects to follow.

We do not talk about banking. Or politics. Mostly, we discuss the bombing missions—Ben evaluates the results of our efforts. And the Pacific war in general. And what we did before the Air Force got us. He was at Yale, spent his last summer as a civilian bicycling through Europe. I was at Bennington College that summer of 1942, with the Graham Dance Company, earning my room and board by rehearsing and performing with the Company, waiting to be called to active duty by the Air Force. When I attempt to describe the thrill of being on stage, hearing the applause, he compresses his thin lips, raises an eyebrow and smiles. I wonder what he is thinking? Ben has never seen a play or attended a symphony concert, a ballet or dance performance. Very strange, I think, for someone from a family so privileged.

I am admittedly curious and envious about the life Ben describes, especially the parties and dances and midnight swims in pools overlooking the Hudson. He says he regularly writes to five of these poolside slow-dancing partners. All "came out" with his younger sister shortly before he traded his white linen suits for suntans. He says he would never marry any one of them. All five or none, he insists.

I do not impress Ben with my tales of Greenwich Village's "far" side. He freely admits to a preference for the other Greenwich, the one in Connecticut, where he can play polo at grandmother's "Overlook Farm."

* * *

We have just been informed that Rest Leave has officially ended. All four squadrons of the Group will move to Munda, New Georgia, during the day tomorrow. We are to take all personal gear and equipment, and our tent, in the plane with us. Reason for the move? Munda is one hour closer to Rabaul than Koli.

NEW GEORGIA

This massive island in the Western Solomons boasts the world's largest enclosed lagoon and, some say, the most beautiful. Certainly it must be the least visited. Called Marovo, it is created by a string of tiny tree-covered coral islets that parallel some 70 miles of the east coast. A crocodile-infested swamp separates the lagoon from the island itself.

A smaller, more conventionally formed lagoon, Roviana, protects the southern coast, extending west from Kalena Bay to Munda Point, site of a strategically located Japanese-built airfield. The allies decided they needed this airfield, and it was the primary objective of a June 30, 1943, invasion by the then untried US 43rd Division.

The Japanese built Munda Airfield in late 1942 on the site of the Lambetti coconut plantation. Legend has it that the tops of coconut trees were secured to suspended wires, the trunks then cut away, permitting work on the runway below to proceed undetected. "Nonsense!" says Pete who was out there at the time. "We knew what they were doing. We bombed hell out of the place!"

Munda Airfield did not succumb until August 5th, a month behind schedule. Two additional divisions were ultimately required to help the US 43rd, which had soon encountered jungle fighting at its worst. It took 50,000 US soldiers to wipe out 9,000 Japanese, at a cost of 1,150 US dead, 4,100 wounded. And we were only 200 miles closer to our primary objective, Rabaul.

Munda, New Georgia, February 15—Our camp at this base is on a rise that overlooks the airstrip and harbor through remnants of battle torn jungle. Although crushed coral paths now connect the tents, the scarred trees and occasional unfilled craters constantly remind us of last summer's fierce fighting on this hill. The relatively short tenancy of US forces has not yet destroyed all the place's "naturalness," and we are forever doing battle with lizards, scorpions, centipedes and land crabs—in addition to the omnipresent mosquitoes. One must faithfully dump-out shoes before stepping into them, and shake clothing and bedding daily.

The missions go on as if we had never left Koli Field. Some are indescribably dull, as yesterday's to Rapopo, southeast of Rabaul, notable only for its concrete runways, so rare in this part of the world. Today's bombing of the Boropop airdrome, at the southern end of New Ireland, was somewhat more exciting. We were there to keep its Hamps and Zekes otherwise occupied while New Zealand forces invaded tiny Nissan Island, 90 miles distant. We kept them occupied, all right: they attacked us 15 minutes out from the target like a swarm of irate Yellow Jacket bees. They were *very* aggressive. "Frenisi" suffered the indignity of taking some AA shrapnel in the tail, other planes in more vital parts; but there were no casualties and all planes returned safely.

Once upon a time it did not take the threat of death to excite me. I wonder if my callouses show?

* * *

The days since Auckland are passing very slowly. Counting them is heartbreaking.

Munda, New Georgia, February 17—Martha writes that she's working on a new dance and that Hindemith is to do the score. Chavez was supposed to, but never sent in any music. Martha's re-reading *Lear*, studying it from Cordelia's point of view, in preparation of a script. Says the Elizabeth Sprague Coolidge Foundation is underwriting the project. I'm reminded of the one time I heard that lady's name mentioned:

> *It's a Sunday night in May 1937, and I'm in the dorm room of a fellow resident of Siebecker House, at the University of Wisconsin. John Coolidge is his name. We're listening to selections from his vast collection of classical records. Though not close friends, we do share an interest in music, and both of us play in the University orchestra: John, cello; I, the bassoon.*
> *We talk about our plans for the summer vacation, about to begin. I tell him*

I'll be working, probably at the cheese curing plant, where I was last summer. John says his grandmother sent him a $250 check and invited him to drive out to California to visit her. But his brother, who's at Harvard, suggested the two of them do a bicycle tour of the British Isles. John says he's decided to do that; his grandmother won't mind so long as they take in all the music festivals. Music is her main interest in life, he says; she's always giving money to composers and orchestras. He wondered if I had heard of her: Elizabeth Sprague Coolidge? I had not.

Munda, New Georgia, February 18—Today's strike was to Vunakanau Air-drome, only seven miles from Rabaul Town, an Australian Air Force field before the war. Concrete runways, like Rapopo. We made our landfall over Ralvana Point on Blanche Bay. The gunners swiveled their turrets side to side, then slowly up and down, firing off a few test rounds at drifting clouds. Our fighter cover, Marine Corsairs, appeared as if by magic and began doing little sashays off our wingtips to get our attention and let us know they were ready. When the black smoke-puffs began to appear up ahead, I knew we were expected. I instinctively sucked in my breath, tightened my buttocks, began to sweat. Then the bombardier took control of the plane, held it straight and level for the bomb run. I felt "Frenisi" shudder when the bomb-bay doors slid open. "Bombs away!" the bombardier shouted over the intercom, then, more quietly, said, "Your plane," to Midthun and me.

It was just then I saw the Zeke. He was at 11 o'clock, high, and streaking down towards the formation. Two Corsairs came charging in from the rear. The Zeke broke his dive and climbed back up into the sun. I maneuvered "Frenisi" in closer to the formation. We were out over Blanche Bay and heading south. The Zeke was back, now below us, at 4 o'clock, and closing in. All our guns were firing at him. Then a Corsair pounced, animal-like, from above and behind. The Zeke kept coming but he was now trailing smoke. Who hit him? The Zeke was trying to climb, still smoking. A Corsair was closing in. The Zeke's upward spiral slowed; then he stalled, a wing dropped and the inevitable uncontrolled cartwheel began: wing over wing, down and down, ending, I knew, in an unseen, unheard, slow-motion splash into the Bay far below.

The Corsairs streaked back to our right flank, waggled their wings and departed, perhaps to go hunting the little black barges that sometimes skim across Rabaul's Simpson Harbor and scatter like waterbugs at the sound of our planes, tracing graceful loops and "S's" on the glassy, dark surface.

* * *

This was only my ninth strike but I am now able to shift my mind during missions into a virtual non-involvement mode. I fly as if by rote, function like an automaton. I am aware of everything happening, but I am no longer a participant: I am an Observer, a Spectator.

I attempted to explain this to Martha. She understood:

> "You describe the sensation of stage when you speak of yourself as a Spectator . . . it is the state of non-feeling that in some way is the highest condition of feeling . . . when people ask me what I feel on the stage I can only truthfully answer—I think I feel nothing."

Munda, New Georgia, February 20—I'm spending the morning on my cot, happy to feel irrelevant for a change. Those less content are strolling, in pairs or small groups, along the winding, white coral paths. Their boots make a crunching sound on the coral. They're on their way to the chapel tent. It's Sunday. I like its quietness and purposeless rhythm.

My tentmates, like me, are not tempted by the chapel, but I don't know why. Such matters are never discussed. In fact, nothing very personal is ever discussed in this tent. The four of us have lived within touching distance of one another—on the plane as well as here in the tent—for nearly three months, but I'm still not sure whether Midthun is married or single; if Pete has brothers and sisters—or even a girlfriend. As for Rumsey, I'm not sure he had a life before leaving Massachusetts and joining the Air Corps.

I think of Rumsey as our "reluctant" bombardier, this sullen, overweight six-footer whose baby-smooth face always looks unwashed, his clothes a size too small and eternally soiled. One avoids facing him directly to escape his foul breath. He's a good enough bombardier but takes no pride in being one.

What Pete and I know, but Rumsey never acknowledges, is that he flunked pilot training, refused to try for navigators' school, requested bombardier training as the easiest way to get a commission. Pete knows this because he was at the same primary flying school. According to a rumor at the time, a week before Rumsey was scheduled to solo he began to have an orgasm every time he gunned the ship down the runway for a takeoff. Pete himself washed-out, but for a more likely reason: he simply didn't solo when the schedule said he should.

Pete is the ultimate navigator. He's the squadron's most experienced and most skilled. He does not discuss his 40-plus missions when sober. One must look deep into Pete's eyes to detect a smile. He challenges new co-pilots like me with dour pronouncements: "No one ever *really* goes home. Ever!" His face is expressionless, even when discussing his favorite writer, Faulkner. (He and I are the only "readers" in the tent.) He wears very small shoes and appears to walk on the balls of his feet. He smokes Camels incessantly. On a mission, when we ask him for a course, he glances at the folded chart clutched in his left hand, takes the pencil from behind his ear and points. Once we have the plane aimed in that direction, he will say: "Keep her right there." We do.

Pete never carries a .45 on missions. He once explained why. Last spring, a newly arrived navigator found an empty cot in Pete's tent and moved in carrying a carbine, like an infantryman. He claimed the Air Force had temporarily run out of .45s. That night he was assigned a mission and was advised not to take the carbine along so he borrowed a .45. He got his plane lost off Choiseul coming back and they ran out of gas. He crawled back to the bomb bay for the water landing and sat in front of the retracted ball turret. When they hit the water, the turret broke loose and crushed him to death. A few nights later, the fellow who had loaned the .45 was himself assigned a mission, and he borrowed Pete's gun to take along. Coming back from Kahili—it was night, and raining—he plotted a course low over the water, hoping they'd see Carney Field's searchlights in time to pull up. They didn't, and hit Cape Esperance. Everyone killed. Pete said he had to break the chain of bad luck of carrying a borrowed .45, and has not worn one since.

Our pilot, Midthun, talks only about bad flying weather, unsafe airplanes and near-fatal missions. He's survived more than 40 and can recall each one in detail. His small, taut-skinned face is never graced with a smile; his hands, never still, are always clasping or unclasping one another. In the tent, he mostly sits, staring, recounting his missions, like a monk telling his beads. The mission he repeatedly describes for us was flown last July:

> "It was night," he begins. "We were returning to Funafuti from a strike on Tarawa. All of us were running out of fuel. Two of my engines had cut out by the time I saw the Funafuti searchlights. I missed the final approach turn, knew I'd never make it around a second time, so did a 'one-eighty' and simply brought her in, downwind, directly in the path of those other

guys trying to land properly. They missed me—I missed them. Skidded off the runway. Down and safe."

Pete says he thinks Midthun "lost it" that night.

There are six other members of the crew, of course: the enlisted men who fire the guns. One is also the radio operator, another doubles as flight engineer. They live together in a tent about a half-mile from ours. We never visit their tent, they never approach ours. Our only common ground is the plane. Tex, the flight engineer, is the only one who initiates a conversation. Invariably it begins: "Another lousy day, huh, Lieutenant?"

* * *

Today's War News Headline: "MARINES INVADE ENIWETOK"

Munda, New Georgia, February 21—Lakunai Airfield, today's target, was once Rabaul Town's municipal airport. It was operated by the Australians until the Japanese came. Lakunai sits on the edge of Simpson Harbor, at the southern end of town, pointing in the direction of the volcano "Matupit," a canoe-paddle away, across a small lagoon. The runway, reportedly, is still surfaced with a mixture of sand and volcanic ash, as it has been since "Matupit" erupted in 1937. So we were told at last night's briefing. We know, of course, that Rabaul is surrounded by five volcanos, because we have flown over them all at various times.

This morning, Pete took us to Lakunai from the east, over the volcano called "The Mother." As the formation turned to the southeast for the bomb-run, one lone Zeke came up to look us over; perhaps to give the Jap anti-aircraft batteries our altitude and direction. He high-tailed it out before we could get a shot at him.

If he gave the AA gunners our position, they still miscalculated. The stuff they sent up didn't come close to hitting anyone.

* * *

A letter today from Martha telling me that an old friend of hers, Ralph Jester, now a major in the Air Force, is in New York following a recent visit to the South Pacific. Told her he knows my outfit and where we are based—but would not tell her! He's with a photographic outfit. He once taught art at Bennington College, then worked in production at one of the Hollywood studios before joining the Air Force.

Martha told of a time she received a telegram from Jester while at Bryn

Mawr to give a lecture. Jester was stationed in Washington. She said the telegram went something like this:

> Darling, you must stay with me when you come to Washington. I can offer you room and bath and breakfast in bed and my undying devotion.

Martha said the telegram was read to her over the telephone by a "spinsterish sounding operator" from the college.

Munda, New Georgia, February 23—The "Whisky Express," direct from Sydney, Australia, arrived earlier today with its precious cargo of booze and fresh food. Bomber Command sends a plane every couple of months, whenever a courier flight is needed—or can be justified, and a B-24 can be spared. Charlie Ott, with whom I flew my first two missions last November, was this plane's pilot. He's through flying combat and is awaiting orders sending him home.

In addition to liquor, Ott brought back some fresh meat (lamb or mutton, whichever), several cases of fresh eggs, and, unexpectedly, enough fresh milk for a glass per man at one meal. All this rare food will be gone in a matter of days but remembered and talked about, and written home about, for months.

The liquor will disappear almost as quickly. Each officer is entitled to purchase only two bottles, at $2.50 each. We list first and second choices and pay in advance. Scotch and gin were my first choices and I got both.

The kind of liquor ordered is not always based on one's taste. Its current trade value is of greater importance to some. Do the possessors (or fabricators) of Japanese souvenirs and native artifacts prefer gin this month? Brandy? I have not seen an authentic native spear or Japanese sword since arriving but the supply still never equals the demand.

I plan to trade my gin to a Marine for a watchband he has fashioned from Australian coins hammered into square links and inset with mother-of-pearl.

Those who choose to drink their liquor allotment tonight will inevitably find their way to the flight line in the morning for a transfusion of pure oxygen from the supply tanks. The price is a half-pint of most anything containing alcohol. Payable to the crew chief.

Munda, New Georgia, February 24—A letter from Martha today telling about attending Katharine Cornell's new play, *Lovers and Friends*, co-starring Raymond Massey. She called the play "absolute drivel," but thought Cornell "ravishing." She said Helen Keller also attended the opening, also as Cornell's guest, and sat in the star's dressing room during the performance. Martha wrote that later, at Cornell's dinner party, Keller had two Old Fashioneds, steak and lots of other things, and three glasses of wine.

I was reminded of the time Keller came to Martha's studio at 66 Fifth Avenue to "watch" a class. She and Martha sat up front, on directors' chairs, their backs to the mirrors, facing those of us taking the class. At the end, Martha had Merce do *pliés* and "jumps-in-place" while Keller held her hands on his waist and laughed and made gurgling noises of delight at the experience of "seeing" Merce jump.

Munda, New Georgia, February 27—Today we bombed, of all things, a group of buildings which formerly housed a Catholic mission center. They are now barracks for Japanese airmen, in the town of Vunapope, whose name, appropriately enough, means "Place of the Catholics." It is located twelve miles southeast of Rabaul on the shores of Blanche Bay.

Some of us also dropped thousand-pounders on wharves jutting out into the Bay. Nearby were entrances to the one-time water tunnels into which Jap barges would disappear when chased by "Pappy" Boyington's Corsairs—until the Navy skipped torpedos into these secret lairs, forever ending these games of hide-and-seek.

Bomber Command estimates that only 33 Jap planes still remain at the five airfields in the Rabaul area. We saw none in the air or on the ground at Tobera and Rapopo, the only fields we had a look at.

* * *

Our departure from Munda this morning was marred by an accident on the runway. "Frenisi" was leading the mission, and we were in the air, circling overhead, waiting for the rest of the squadron to come up and join us, when a column of black smoke suddenly began rising from the field. The Tower said a plane had blown a tire on takeoff, swerved to the side, hit a gas truck, setting off a big fire. We were told to proceed to Rabaul with the planes already in the air.

Six hours later, as we prepared to land back on Munda, I could see bulldozers still working alongside the airstrip, pushing piles of smoking, twisted metal, filling large holes with crushed coral. We learned at debriefing that it was O'Toole's plane that blew the tire and rammed the gas truck. O'Toole and his crew had arrived at Munda just last week. This was to have been their first mission. Pete and I had gone to O'Toole's tent last night with a little whiskey to wish them luck.

The way I heard the story, the crew members jumped clear of the plane the moment it came to rest after hitting the truck. Smoke and flames could already be seen rising from a section of the right wing. O'Toole counted heads: the flight engineer was missing. O'Toole ran back to the plane to look for him. He found him on the catwalk in the bomb bay, where he always stood during takeoff. He was wedged in between two metal stanchions which had been twisted out of place by the collision with the truck. The six one-thousand pound bombs the plane was carrying were on racks behind the twisted stanchions. O'Toole could not get the engineer loose. The engineer begged O'Toole to shoot him. O'Toole could not do that. He said he'd go back outside for help. They both knew there wasn't time for that. The fire would get to the gas tanks any second.

O'Toole crawled back up to the top escape hatch and jumped to the ground. Broke his ankle. The crew members rushed to pull him back from the burning plane. They asked if he had found the engineer. He said he had but that it was too late.

The crew sat there just off the tarmac staring at the burning plane. Then a gas tank blew. Flames quickly enveloped the entire plane. Moments later, one of the bombs exploded. Then, one by one, the other five went off.

Munda, New Georgia, March 1—Eleven missions are by now embedded in my memory: unending journeys through barren skies in search of islands beyond the horizon. I am always high over a wasteland of seas, forever tracing the edge of a threatening storm. The target I seek is hidden beneath the mottled green-brown jungle mat far below—until it is betrayed by staccato flashes of fire triggered by the shadows of my plane's wings. Wisps of smoke from exploding aerial shells now brush the windscreen.

The roar of the straining engines fills the cabin; unintelligible radio signals crackle in my headphones. I feel I'm becoming a part of the plane; I depend upon it for life.

I breathe only when attached to the plane's oxygen system. My heart beats only if the propellers are turning. I hear only when the radio is turned on. The plane's wings are my arms; the Automatic Pilot is my brain.

But who am I? A skin-tight leather helmet hides my hair and forehead. Dark-paned sunglasses conceal the color and shape of my eyes. The rubber oxygen mask, moulded to the contours of my nose and mouth, disguises my face. The color of my skin, my race, my sex are not discernable.

I wear a large steel "flak helmet." It is my "Perseus Cap." It renders me invisible to Zekes and Zeros.

Munda, New Georgia, March 2—The Officers Club was not open for business when I walked by this afternoon but Russ, the GI bartender, was inside taking inventory or something, and I talked him into selling me a beer. Said it might get me in the mood for the fried Spam, or whatever we'll get for dinner, always served promptly at 4:30. I asked if he knew why we eat so early? He didn't, but said not everyone out here eats at 4:30, or eats Spam every day.

I knew this was my cue to ask who he was talking about. I chat often enough with Russ to know when I'm supposed to ask questions. Our little talks at the bar are mostly about New York—more specifically, Greenwich Village. He lived on 14th Street, west of 8th Avenue—the Village suburbs, I tell him. My $5 a week hall bedroom was at 65 Charles Street, a more legitimate Village address.

I asked the question: Who out here doesn't eat Spam for dinner at 4:30? Guys like the ones I bartendered for at a party last Friday, he answered. Said the job was arranged by the Mess Sergeant; paid 25 bucks minus five for the Sergeant. Russ promised not to talk about it or who he saw there.

Russ seemed eager to break his promise and I did not discourage him. Said he found the tent in the Group Officers area. Had a ship's bell hanging on a post outside. He clanged the bell and a GI wearing a white waiter's jacket opened the door flaps. Wanted to know if Russ was a guest or the bartender. Bartender, Russ said, and was invited inside.

The waiter pointed to a portable bar but said nothing, then resumed setting the long, cloth-covered table that took up most of the floor space. Russ said it was only then he realized that the inside of the tent was completely lined with what looked like white silk. None of the canvas was showing. The place looked like a boudoir, Russ said. Long, overlapping panels of the silk were hung from the peak and somehow fastened to the sides of the tent to form pleated sidewalls. He figured the material was parachute silk.

An oriental-type rug hid the floor; two cots, covered with batik spreads and piled with colorful, overstuffed pillows, were pushed up against the white silk sidewalls. Several footlockers, disguised with fabrics and woven-grass mats, served as coffee tables. A wooden wheel-type candelabra hung over the dining table. There were cloth napkins, silverware and a wine glass at each place setting.

Russ said the little portable bar had everything he needed—ice, plain water, soda, tonic, even lemons and limes, in addition to beer and the most expensive brands of the usual selection of booze.

The colonel hosting the affair arrived moments later with two other officers. He asked Russ his name, said he hoped he had everything he needed in the bar. Russ assured him he did and took the officers' drink order: two gins, one scotch, all doubles on the rocks. The GI waiter served the drinks.

A master sergeant and two buck privates arrived next. The sergeant said "Hi!" to the colonel as if they were old friends but did not introduce the privates who, Russ said, appeared stunned by this candle-lit, silk-lined tent. The sergeant asked Russ for a beer; the privates ordered gin with tonic water. The waiter served the drinks.

Russ said he was kept busy making drinks for the next hour or so. The waiter passed plates of cheese and nuts. A little after 8:00, the colonel, rather abruptly, Russ thought, said everyone should drink up, that dinner would be ready in about five minutes. He then went over to the bar and told Russ he could leave as soon as he had straightened up, that they'd help themselves from then on, and the waiter would serve the wine. He held out some folded bills, said thank you and good night.

As Russ left the tent he saw the waiter unloading some large covered containers from the back of a Jeep. He figured it was the dinner, probably prepared by the Mess Sergeant.

* * *

Russ wondered if I had any idea what happened in that silk-lined tent after he left. I said I had some ideas. I said I didn't think those men were there to plan an invasion; or that it was the weekly meeting of the Munda Rotary Club. I asked Russ to get me another beer while I thought about it.

Munda, New Georgia, March 6—Today's mission took us to Kavieng, at the tip of New Ireland, a long, narrow, club-shaped island extending 200 miles to the northwest from the vicinity of Rabaul. Our target was Panapei, a satellite field of Kavieng Airdrome. Kavieng is considered a major Japanese military port and base, second only to Rabaul, but no fighters challenged us, and the anti-aircraft fire was erratic.

The glimpse I had of Kavieng's harbor convinced me that sailboats would be more appropriate in that setting than the warships and barges lurking off-shore.

Most conspicuous from the air is what Pete identified as the "Boluminski Highway" snaking its way south from Kavieng the length of the island, which is seldom more than three miles wide. Ben told me tonight that the highway dates back to pre-WWI days when Germany owned the place. Boluminski was Chief Administrator and got the highway built—and named for himself. Today it is a busy truck route for moving supplies off-loaded at Kavieng and destined for Rabaul. The Corsairs based at Torokina on Bougainville would love to go truck hunting along this road but it is too distant for their limited fuel supply.

Pete took us over the Green Islands on the return trip to Munda. An airstrip is being built on Nissan, the largest island in the group. Nissan was taken by New Zealand troops less than a month ago. Ben says the Kiwis were told to expect 100 Jap defenders. They encountered 102. All were dead within five days of the invasion. The entire native population of 1200 has since been evacuated to Guadalcanal for the duration of the war. Someone decided there was not enough room for the native villages and gardens and our airfield.

* * *

We read in "Yank" magazine that a movie called *Casablanca* won this year's Academy Award. Needless to say, it has not yet played the South Pacific circuit.

Munda, New Georgia, March 8—Today was our sixth consecutive strike to Rabaul, but the first in months without fighter escort. Reason is that no Jap fighters have been seen thereabouts for a week. We've been told they were pulled back to Truk. Anti-aircraft fire heavy as always at Rapapo Airdrome, where we dropped our bombs on a barracks complex.

I didn't miss the Zekes and Hamps today but I did the Marine Corsairs Pappy Boyington and his "Black Sheep" squadron flew to escort our planes these past several months. Even after Pappy got himself shot down last January, the Corsairs were always there, and always a delight to watch: their cocky little sashays off the flank of the formation; the mock feints to make-believe tap our wingtips. At times they were in so close I could read the team name on the baseball caps the pilots wore.

We were at 23,000, ringed by those innocent looking puffs of black smoke from the anti-aircraft fire, when, without explanation, Rumsey salvoed the whole bomb load. He just let 'em go. Midthun put us into a steep left turn to get us out of there. Made a complete circle but the exploding shells followed us all the way.

When we finally got back out over the water, away from those guns,

Midthun eased off on the throttles. When we were down to 15,000 I told the crew they could take off their oxygen masks. And got a damage report: "Holes in left rudder." "Piece of cowling off #2 engine." "#4 spilling oil. Hit by flak?" "Any coffee left?"

Midthun said to take us home. I grabbed the wheel. Before I could light a cigarette, Midthun was asleep. Pete came forward and squatted beside my seat. "Keep her at 160 degrees," he said. Just as we were leaving Cape Gazelle, he pointed down to the water. "Where Pappy Boyington got it," he said. "Made a water-landing O.K. but a Jap sub was right there. Pulled him aboard."

Oil pressure on No. 4 kept dropping so I feathered it and we went home on three.

Munda, New Georgia, March 10—I attended the movie *My Sister Eileen* tonight for the third time since coming to the South Pacific. I keep going back to savor the few glimpses of New York's Greenwich Village I miss so much: the crown of roof gardens high above Gay Street; the brightly painted fire escapes scaling brownstones on West 11th Street; the de Chirico-like stillness of Waverly Place.

Those scenes remain in the back of my eyes as I look out at the lights of other tents in the camp, dim and flickering through the webs of hanging vines. Night mists rise like twisting tentacles. And I hear the now-familiar, queer little chirps and squeals, the sad, brief, three-note songs of sleepy birds; and the insistent drones of unknown insects. Occasionally the darkness is pierced by a human-like scream which instantly quiets all other creatures.

But tonight the sudden, unexpected intrusion that hushed the jungle sounds was the clear, liquid trill of a flute signalling for attention. After a brief pause, a simple two-bar melody echoed through the stilled night. The flute repeated the phrase, then played it a third time an octave higher, now accompanied by a harmonica chromatically sliding up and down the scale. A heavily strummed guitar joined in from another tent, soon to be followed by the sweet, constricted moan of a saxophone. Hand-claps and foot-stomps provided a beat. A chorus of male voices, coming from all sections of the camp, gave words to the familiar tune. All the tents were now lighted.

When the song ended, the guitar introduced another. The flute and harmonica and saxophone quickly joined in. An even greater number of voices sang the words or simply hummed the tune.

Song followed song. In less than half an hour, the impromptu concert ended as if on cue. There were a few tentative strums on the guitar, a quiet arpeggio from the flute; then silence. One by one, the tent lights blinked off. Once again I heard only the chirps and squeals, the brief songs of sleepy birds. I had returned to the island of New Georgia. Waverly Place would be re-visited in dreams.

Munda, New Georgia, March 13—The footlocker I so carefully packed at Hamilton Field last November caught up with me today. It holds all the personal flying gear I could not bring with me on the flight over because of weight limitations: an oxygen mask specially molded to fit the contours of my face; a hand-stitched, skin-tight leather flying helmet; fleece-lined boots and jacket; and the wool dress uniforms left behind at a cleaners in Tucson.

The stuff all seems so irrelevant now. I've been using an oxygen mask tossed to me by a supply clerk and it has worked fine on 14 missions to date. Instead of a fancy leather helmet, I wear a long-visored cap of much-washed khaki, stitched up for me by a parachute rigger. And the flight deck heaters make fleece-lined clothes unnecessary.

Another trunk, holding a bed roll, full field equipment, my personal parachute, a jungle survival kit, also packed by me that November day at Hamilton, is presumably still on the high seas.

* * *

I was promoted today to 1st Lieutenant which entitles me to a monthly salary of $296. After deductions for rations, insurance, a $25 war bond, and $100 to a savings account, I'll have $145 in "walking around" money— and no place to spend it. Only PX supplies and beer can be purchased with dollars. Liquor is the preferred currency for anything of value. We get paid in cash, and I keep my bills in a cigar box, for use, hopefully, on the next trip to Auckland.

Air medals were handed out to one and all the other day. The "price" is surviving five missions. I have 14 so I got a medal and a cluster. One more mission and I get another cluster. ("Frenisi" has 63 missions to date.)

Munda, New Georgia, March 14—Midthun and Rumsey have gone home. The orders came suddenly, unexpectedly, while everyone was at breakfast this morning. By noon, they were on a flight to Guadalcanal to connect with the plane that will take them to San Francisco. No time for a proper send-off. But, of course, most of their friends—except for Pete—have long since gone back. Or down.

The only explanation for Pete not getting his orders, I'm told, is the shortage of navigator replacements.

Our new first pilot is Bob Murphy, who's been co-piloting in the 424th Squadron for almost a year. Seems very well-adjusted for someone with so much time out here. No hang-ups I could discover during the couple of hours we spent together at the club.

Ron Hunter comes from the same 424th crew but appears to be a very different kind of guy: very quiet, serious, the typical "loner." Murphy says he's a first-rate bombardier but does not much care for flying.

Munda, New Georgia, March 18—These early spring mornings are being squandered on bravado forays to Fortress Rabaul. One of its five airfields is the usual target; on rare occasions, a warship astray on Blanche Bay. Today, it is the town itself: specifically, the commercial wharves, "Customs Wharf," "Burns-Philip Wharf," and "New Wharf." All hug the crescent-shaped downtown quay. (Built by the Germans, before WWI, says Ben.)

It was my 17th strike but the first with civilian casualties a certainty. And, ironically, I was to fly it as first pilot not co-pilot. Murphy did not tell me this until we had begun the climb to altitude, and were less than an hour out from the target. Too late to change seats as we were already hooked up to oxygen. I would have to fly from the co-pilot's side. No matter. All the "hard" decisions would be mine to make. If we got badly shot up, do I order everyone to bail out? What if someone is wounded and can't jump? Let the others jump and attempt a water landing with the wounded guy? And any volunteers? If we lose an engine—or maybe two—do I try to stay with the group or head for home?

These were among my thoughts as I took over the controls and began maneuvering "Frenisi" to its place in the formation. We were at 20,000 feet, over the west coast of Bougainville. I could see New Britain on the horizon. I was excited—proud and confident, a little anxious. I supressed all thoughts of civilians in the target area.

We made our landfall on Crater Peninsula, coming in from the north-east, over St. George Channel. I saw a volcano off the right wing. "North Daughter," Pete said. The empty cone on our left was "The Mother," he said. We were where we were supposed to be. Directly ahead was Lakunai Airfield, at the edge of town. Where were the Zekes? I struggled to get "Frenisi" straight and level. It mushed and skidded at this altitude no matter how much rudder I used. Would it roll over if I leaned too far to the side? When I finally had it right, I called Hunter to take over for the bomb run. Moments later I heard his shouted "Bombs away!" on the intercom. "Frenisi" shuddered as the first stick of bombs fell out. Murphy pointed to the puffs of black smoke up ahead: the anti-aircraft guns were on our altitude but way off on range. But no Zekes!

Now Pete was kneeling by my seat, tapping the compass dial at the 140-degree mark. I steepened the turn left and pushed forward on the wheel to increase our speed. When the compass read 140, Pete pointed straight ahead and I leveled off. Cape Gazelle was off the right wing. Munda was still three hours farther on. It was then I remembered I had forgotten to look down when we dropped the bombs. I never even saw our target, the wharves.

* * *

Murphy said I did good, keeping "Frenisi" right on course through the anti-aircraft fire. I did not tell him how scared I was. Or that when Hunter released the bombs I briefly closed my eyes and whispered into my oxygen mask, "Miss the people . . . please!"

Tonight, on my cot, under the mosquito net shroud, I shall re-fly the mission again, alone, and remember those silent witnesses on the ground, cowering from the columns of swirling smoke and fire that marked the path of our bombs dropped so deliberately this early spring morning on that once and always pretty little tropical village called Rabaul.

Koli, Guadalcanal, March 23—The squadron is back at the 'Canal, temporarily on rest leave. I flew eight strikes in the past 15 days, including six to Rabaul. Bomber Command decided we were due some time on the ground.

One of those strikes I will not soon forget: yesterday's to Kahili, on the southern coast of Bougainville. This is the notorious air base from which Japanese fighters and bombers, a year ago, were bombing and strafing US positions on Guadalcanal at will. It became a major target for our bombers—a formidable target, defended by hundreds of Jap fighters and dozens of anti-aircraft batteries. We may have lost more planes over Kahili than at any other Jap base in the South Pacific. Still counting at Rabaul . . .

* * *

The "old timers," including Pete, refer to their first few months out here as "When Kahili was rough!" Kahili was still "rough" yesterday morning. We were at 21-thousand feet, on the bomb run, over the airfield. I saw the flash of an explosion under the plane up ahead—we had a clear view of its belly from our stepped-down position to the right and below.

Murphy grabbed my arm. As we stared, the plane's ball turret suddenly came loose from the ring that held it to the plane. The stainless steel sphere slowly fell away, rotating, then spinning, falling, faster and faster . . . I thought of the man inside in his crouched position, jammed against the sides of the twirling steel coffin. Was he screaming?

"When Kahili was rough . . . when Kahili was rough . . ."

* * *

The Mess Hall bulletin board carries an announcement of Marines landing on tiny Emirau island, 90 miles northwest of Kavieng. Needed as an emergency landing option when and if we begin flying missions to Truk—700 miles farther on—says Ben. The only opposition to the landing came from a handful of natives proclaiming themselves Seventh Day Adventists.

* * *

While standing in the communal open-air shower this afternoon, I watched a large, silver transport plane slowly descend from the sky and majestically glide above our tents for a landing at Koli. I recognized it as one of the C-54s we've heard so much about—the newest, largest, fastest transport plane ever built. We're told it flies from San Francisco to Guadalcanal in 38 hours with only two fuel stops en route. And returns to San Francisco the next day with men who have finished flying their missions. My heart aches at the thought of this beautiful plane leaving tomorrow without me!

During dinner, later, several bags of mail from that same plane were brought to the Mess Hall. There were five letters for me. And D. H. Lawrence's *Sons and Lovers*, sent by Franny Benn Hall.

Koli, Guadalcanal, March 24—Another piece of mail for me arriving on that C-54 was the November 1943 issue of the University of Wisconsin's *Alumnus* magazine. I found only two names I recognized as members of my 1940 Class: Edwin Newman, now a Naval Ensign in Communications, stationed at Trinidad; and Farrington Daniels, Jr., currently a fourth year medical student at Harvard. The three of us lived in Siebecker House at the Mens Dorms on the shores of Lake Mendota in Madison.

Newman was in charge of producing the editorial page of the student newspaper, *Daily Cardinal*, and from time to time gave me books to review for the paper. Knowing I was anxious to increase my writing experience, he also agreed to let me write the weekly Dance News column and review performances—if the head of the Dance Department, Margaret H'Doubler, approved. She did, but only after I agreed to take dance classes. This opportunity, and the experience gained, led to my winning a scholarship to the annual Summer School of the Dance at Bennington College in the summer of 1940, where I met Martha Graham and joined her Company. Writing about dance, I quickly learned, was not nearly as exciting as the dancing itself, and I decided to postpone the writing career.

Daniels' parents lived in Madison—his father was a professor in the Chemistry department—but they wanted Farrington to have the experience of living on campus. Ed, Farrington, and I were good friends.

It is a Sunday night in 1936 and the late October moon shadows the sidewalk with traceries of elm leaves. Farrington knows the neighborhood and quickly finds the small Unitarian church where Norman Thomas will speak.

Inside, most of the front pews are empty and we take seats in the center, close to the lectern. I stare at the tall, white-haired man who seems to be staring back at each of us, one at a time. Suddenly he begins speaking, at the same time striding back and forth, the heels of his high-top black shoes hammering the wooden floor. His deep, gravely, bass voice booms, thunders, echoes in the half-filled nave; his fist strikes the open palm of his left hand at the end of each shouted sentence.

I cringe as if the words themselves are striking me, watching his long finger jabbing and pointing and shaking in my direction. I press back against the pew to escape the pronouncements he hurls like epithets: "This war in Europe—we'll soon be in it! You'll be in it! Soon enough! And do you know where it'll end? I'll tell you: on some godforsaken island in the Pacific, that's where! And you men—you students—you'll be there, on that godforsaken island! Fighting for your life! Wondering how you got there. And why!"

Farrington and I do not leave immediately after the lecture. We are reluctant to approach Thomas for fear he might question us. We leaf through the pamphlets displayed on a table near the door. We each put a few coins in a Contributions Box, then leave the church wearing lapel pins reading Socialists for Peace.

I showed Pete the *Alumnus* magazine and told him about the Thomas lecture. "Damn!" he said. "That old bastard! Said we'd end up out here!" Then we headed for the Club to help celebrate a 23-year-old "Old Boy's" promotion to captain. I attempted a few Graham "sits," as befitted the occasion. My "sit" was more a "fall," but no one seemed to notice.

Koli, Guadalcanal, March 29—Franny writes to tell me that MacMillian is sponsoring a novel writing contest for servicemen. Deadline is December 31. First prize, $2,500. And instant fame.

I don't really have a novel in mind but hope one of these days to get started on the story of Gwicky and his three tentmates, the guys who briefly lived in the tent across from ours, who kept us awake the night before what turned out to be their last mission, only their fourth. Shot down, all killed, off Poporang.

Wonder what they were celebrating that last night?

I learned from Ben the next day that their plane, the "Mary-Jane," was named by Gwicky for his wife Mary, *and* girlfriend, Jane. He no doubt learned many things about Gwicky and his tentmates. Ben was assigned to collect and send home the personal effects of all four officers. He had to read all their letters and diaries and so on to make sure the "wrong" pieces of paper were not sent home. He has told me much of what he learned.

In my story, I would make Ben the Narrator. First person? Third person? Haven't decided. I'd have him spend an entire night in the empty tent, sorting through all the personal stuff. He'd make little piles on each man's cot: one pile for the things it would be safe to send home to a mother, a wife, a girlfriend. A father. Another pile for "burning," as Ben would say. The man's family would not know the person this pile represented. The man's Air Force buddies would possibly not recognize the man from either pile.

As Ben continued his probing of the dreams and fears and hopes of these four unfinished lives, one by one the other tent lights switched off, and the darkness became filled with sounds of night: a screech, a flutter of large wings, a clucking that accelerates into a whine, drone-songs of insects, the nervous yelping of some animal in distress. Later, when the moon was higher overhead and the shadows sharper, there were voices of men talking while they slept—short cries for help, a gasp, a swallowed "No!" from a nightmare.

Shortly before dawn, Ben would hear the shriek of the wake-up whistle in the doorways of those who would be flying today, and later watch the silent file of men slowly moving along the crushed gravel paths to the mess hall. He would then lie down on one of the cots in the empty tent, pushing aside the little pile of secrets he was guarding, but not close his eyes to sleep until he heard the first planes take off.

* * *

I have not yet made notes or even written a line of the story. Nor have I been able to work on the project Martha suggested, a script for a possible collaboration with Sam Barber on a new dance. She said to ". . . talk to someone across a distance about anything, everything . . ." This I do, in many of my letters, but the words are not yet my "deaths and entrances" that they must be to please her.

Munda, New Georgia, April 5—Rest Leave ended abruptly yesterday morning—along with any hope of re-visiting Auckland—by an order sending us back here to Munda to attend an urgent "special" briefing. The unsettling first announcement is that tomorrow we will be taking off on a 1600 mile roundtrip night bombing mission to Truk, legendary headquarters of the Japanese Imperial Combined Fleet.

We are told that daylight raids on Truk by other 13th Air Force squadrons last month resulted in losses so great that night missions were ordered. The one scheduled for tomorrow will be the first, and "Frenisi" and its crew are on the list to go. We will stage from tiny Nissan, 400 miles closer to Truk, in the Green Islands group.

As the Briefers explained, Truk is actually a cluster of small islands inside a coral reef which forms a lagoon 140 miles in circumference. Our targets tomorrow night will be on Dublon Island, in the eastern part of the lagoon. There's a seaplane base there, a submarine base, as well as military warehouses, docks, tank farms and barracks. No airfield, but defending aircraft by the hundreds, including night fighters, are close by, on aircraft carriers and neighboring islands.

We fly to Nissan in the morning.

Nissan Island, April 7—I am awakened by an early morning shower. It drums a muted tattoo on the canvas roof. An onshore breeze carries faint scents of the sea through the open-sided tent. The doorway fills with glints of the rising sun made less harsh by the mosquito net draped over my cot.

The others sleep on. My eyes are open but I remain in the thrall of last night's mission to Truk.

* * *

It begins at dusk, the lift-off through all the spilled colors of the dying day. Pete has aimed us at a tiny cluster of specks 800 miles to the northnorthwest. He says we should find it about midnight, with or without the help of the radar-equipped "Snooper" planes assigned to lead our formation. (Pete questions their necessity. "All I need are a few stars and an horizon," he grumbles.)

We flew up from Munda in the morning. The final briefing is attended by reporters as well as Air Force brass. And the 23 crews. We are told the strike is "newsworthy" because it is the first ever on Truk at night; and is so long—10½ hours roundtrip. The General adds that the mission is of "immense strategic value—despite its great risks." A wire service reporter stops me on the way out, asks where I'm from, the name of the local newspaper. "*Wisconsin Rapids Tribune*," I say. Wonders how I "feel" about going to Truk? Scared, of course, I tell him, and walk away.

Murphy and I go down to the line to check on "Frenisi." Have the crews topped the gas tanks? Checked the oxygen supply? Hunter is there to supervise the loading of the bombs; Tex, to count the boxes of ammunition at each gun station.

The reporters join us at our late—one cannot help thinking "last"—afternoon dinner of fresh New Zealand lamb and fresh potatoes, and we quickly assure them this is not a typical menu.

Within an hour after takeoff, we're alone in the darkening sky, each plane proceeding on its own, hopefully to rendezvous five hours from now and be in formation before the night fighters come looking for us. Thankfully, there's no weather to contend with, only the darkness to conquer—and those strange, unexplainable distractions which invade the night and must be subdued. (I think of Djuna Barnes' *Nightwood* and her Dr. Matthew-Mighty-grain-of-salt-Dante-O'Connor.)

Murphy and I take turns napping while the other attends to keeping "Frenisi" in the air: checking the Automatic Pilot, the fuel supply, oil pressure and cylinder head temperature of each engine; keeping the props synchronized—by their sound, when one can no longer watch the shadow pattern; scanning the night sky continuously for a flash of light that could portend danger. The sudden moistening of the windscreen is unsettling until I realize we have passed through a cloud.

The intercom is silent—is everyone but me asleep? All planes are observing radio silence, but I switch on the short wave band, hoping to catch some music being beamed from Australia—or even the taunting, giggling voice of "Tokyo Rose" from Japan. Only echoing silence . . .

As soon as a few stars appear, Pete gets his sextant and looks for the North Star. He thinks he can distinguish an horizon. I cannot. A pinhead of light I saw a moment ago—a star, I presumed—now appears below us! But fades from sight as I stare. I'm reminded of a night formation exercise in flight school when I followed an automobile's tail light for several minutes, thinking it was the wing light of the plane leading us.

It is 10:30 when Tex brings coffee and cheese sandwiches to the flight deck. Pete says he knows where we are; that we'll be at the rendezvous in an hour. It's over one of the atolls in the Mortlock group, a hundred miles

The "Frenisi." *Photo courtesy of Kurt Patzlaff. Used with permission.*

The "Frenisi" crew. The author is standing third from the right. *Photo courtesy of Kurt Patzlaff. Used with permission.*

Group photo of "Letter to the World." The author is standing third from the right. *Photo courtesy of Knopf-Pix. Used with permission.*

"Punch and the Judy" photo of David Zellmer and Martha Graham. *Photo courtesy of Arnold Eagle.*

"Punch and the Judy" photo of David Zellmer and Martha Graham. *Photo courtesy of Arnold Eagle.*

from Truk lagoon. I call all the crew members on the intercom and give them the ETA. And tell them to watch for night fighters. The Japs now have a twin engine plane called "Irving" that lobs air-burst phosphorus bombs in the midst of B-24 formations. On one of the last daylight missions to Truk, a '24 trailing gas from a damaged engine was set afire by one of them. Blew up in mid-air. Everyone killed.

When the other planes begin appearing, one by one, they are like shadowy behemoths, reluctantly revealing themselves. And, as if by some primordial herding instinct, they begin closing in and maneuvering for their assigned slots in the bombing formation. I cannot see the Mortlock Islands below but Pete assures me they are there.

"Frenisi" mushes in this thin air at 23,000 feet. I need more and more throttle to keep up with the others. If I back the throttles off, even a little, we lose altitude. I must move the ailerons and rudders twice as far, and hold them twice as long, to change our attitude. We seem balanced on a wire strung between two unseen stars. I feel that if I lean too far to one side, the plane might roll over to its side.

When at last we find our place in the formation—just slightly below and off the right wing of the squadron leader—I feel I have taken a reluctant old race horse into the starting gate one last time. This is "Frenisi's" 69th mission. (My 20th.)

Then we see the stiletto-like searchlight beams piercing our cover of darkness, fingering for us in the sky as if intent on impaling us like butterflies on pins. Tracer-stained anti-aircraft shells stream upward but, miraculously, never find us. The searchlights flood the flight deck with a blinding blue-white light.

We fly on, all 23 planes as one, awaiting Hunter's shout of "bombs away!" We all know there's only 15-minutes allotted to find Dublon, just inside the lagoon, and bomb our targets on the tiny island—the seaplane base, warehouses, docks, hopefully some anti-aircraft guns and searchlights.

I see fires on Dublon, set by the planes up ahead. They reveal the outline of tiny Etan Island, just opposite Dublon Town, whose airfield is the largest of any at Truk. Finally, Hunter shouts "Bombs away!" Murphy begins the steep, banking turn to the right that takes us out of the lagoon.

I stare out my window, searching for night fighters. Our turn is so tight, the plane seems to be pivoting on its right wing. I hear a scream on the intercom: "Bogie! Three o'clock—high!" I see the glow of a night fighter's twin exhausts streak by, then recede into the distance. An Irving, I'm sure. He'll be back.

Murphy rolls us out of the turn and levels off. "Take over!" he tells me. I grab the wheel with both hands, place my boots on the rudder pedals. Pete kneels beside my seat, reaches up to the compass with his pencil and points to 170 degrees. "Keep her right there," he says. I nod as I continue the turn to the new heading.

I can no longer see stars. Clouds must have moved in. No horizon, either. I check the Artificial Horizon when I'm at 170 degrees and leveled off. Looks fine, but I feel we are still in the turn. Artificial Horizon must be wrong; malfunctioning, I'm sure. I *feel* us turning. I rotate the wheel to the left to counter the turn. Murphy immediately leans over, taps the Artificial Horizon case. He grabs the wheel, abruptly rotates it back to the right until the instrument says we're level. He nods to me to take over again.

But a moment later, I feel we are climbing. I'm convinced of it. I push the control column forward and wait. But now the altimeter shows us losing altitude. I no longer know what to do. I feel panicky, sick to my stomach, hot and sweaty. I grab Murphy's arm and tell him to take over. I slide down in my seat until my head is below the window. I cover my eyes with my cap.

Now I feel myself being shaken. Had I fallen asleep? Murphy is yelling for me to look out the window. I sit upright and see a blinding flash . . . an explosion . . . a swirling fireball. It's one of our planes, I know, and it disintegrates as I watch. Burning chunks of fuselage are hurtling in all directions, then slowly tumbling into the darkness below. Tracer shells from our guns streak upwards towards a tiny speck of light moving over-head. It's beyond their range, alas, and soon disappears. The sky is once again empty and dark.

Murphy says he grabbed my arm when he saw the exhaust of the Irving streak into view just above us; knew it was about to lob a bomb.

My vertigo is gone. I tell Murphy I think I can now keep "Frenisi" rightside up. Then take her, he says.

Within minutes, we are again alone in the sky. Each plane is to find its own way back to Nissan. I switch on the radio. This time I hear voices: one of the Snooper planes is calling for a Dumbo to search for possible survivors of the plane we saw blowing up.

Some hours later, the moon makes one final brief, but tantalizing, ap-pearance, then disappears behind a tumble of roiling black clouds. Sheets of rain begin to rake the windscreen. "Frenisi" struggles on, head down, engines whining.

About two hours from when Pete said we'll reach Nissan, the rain stops, clouds thin, and there off the left wing is a huge red-orange sun emerging from the black, white-capped sea. I quickly dip the wing and alert everyone over the intercom to take a look. And sigh.

We do not see the sun, the sky or the sea again until we reach Nissan.

Pete spends the last half hour on his haunches beside my seat, checking his watch, the compass, the airspeed indicator. Then, suddenly, he rises and leans closer to the windscreen, pointing into the wind and rain. "Nissan dead ahead," he pronounces. "Begin your let down." I see only rain and swirling clouds, but ease the throttles back a little.

Minutes later, we see the face of a massive cliff looming through the half-light of the storm—and realize we are too low! Murphy and I frantically pull back on the control column and at the same time jam the throttles full forward. It's as if we're reining "Frenisi" back and kicking her loins to make her leap to the top of the cliff.

She makes it to the top, but clips a perimeter light during the very brief, very shallow glide to the runway. We have to stomp the brakes to get off at the taxiway.

End of first night mission to Truk.

Munda, New Georgia, April 11—O'Toole, who broke a leg jumping from his plane after it blew a tire on takeoff and crashed into a gas truck, is still grounded and wearing a plaster cast. This did not prevent him from taking a P-38 up on a test-hop yesterday. Without permission, of course. The P-38 had been left behind for repairs, now completed, and the crew chief wanted the plane test-flown. O'Toole learned this and volunteered his services, claiming he knew all about P-38s. The crew chief ran him through the cockpit procedure and wished him luck, knowing perfectly well O'Toole was lying. It would have been their own little secret except that O'Toole had to buzz the camp area, and the Major's tent. Kind of low. That ended O'Toole's brief career as a P-38 pilot.

Munda, New Georgia, April 14—Today's scheduled return to Truk was unceremoniously scrubbed by a surprise Jap mortar attack that threatened our airstrips on Bougainville. The squadron had flown to one of the fields, Torokina's Piva Uncle, early yesterday, intending to spend the afternoon there at the Marine base before taking off for our second nighttime visit to that most feared of all our targets.

Some of us were in the Officers Club, waiting for the sun to sink another degree or two before going to dinner, when the screech of a Klaxon horn sent everyone running for cover. We could hear the "thunk" of mortars being fired. Theirs? Ours? We soon learned that Japs had broken through the perimeter protecting the three Torokina airfields. The Marine base commander ordered us and our planes "to hell out of here! Now!"

A truck took us back to the taxiway where we had parked "Frenisi." There we found Hunter, our tall, silent bombardier, calmly toggling loose the entire load of 500-pound bombs, one by one. He had hand-cranked open the bomb bay doors. After he convinced us the bombs were un-armed, we helped roll them into the drainage ditch. Hunter said he had decided that landing the plane a second time in one day with a full load of bombs was asking for it. We agreed.

I asked Hunter how many beers it took to convince him to dump the bombs. No beer, he said. He had been guzzling a fancy new Marine drink: powdered milk in water over shaved ice, heavy on the vanilla extract.

Pete pointed us a way back to Munda around and under the gathering thunderheads. We landed in a driving rainstorm spilling from one of them; but with an empty bomb-bay. And no new Truk nightmares to endure this night.

Munda, New Georgia, April 16—The current issue of *Esquire* carries a photograph that cruelly stirs old memories. It's of Mary Martin and the lead dancers in her Broadway show, *One Touch of Venus*. I cannot resist showing it to Pete and singling out the dancer I once knew so well; or thought I did. I tell him the story of our romance while both of us were dancers in Martha's Company, of its abrupt end at Maxwell Field, Ala-bama, where I was in Pre-Flight Training. I tell him she had come there, alone, all the way from New York on a bus, so we could be married. All arrangements had been made: chaplain booked, best man waiting in the lobby with the flowers. And of learning even before she closed the door to the hotel room that there would not be a marriage.

I tell Pete of the letter I received from Ed Newman, a year of silence later, after I had arrived on Guadalcanal, telling of the long conversation he had with her in New York and her explaining why she had ended our relationship: I am not yet mature, not yet an adult, she said; do not know what I want to do, what I believe in. I am indiscriminate in choosing friends; naive about politics. And I do not really appreciate the fact that she is Jewish.

How did you plead, Pete asks. Guilty on all counts, I tell him. Let's drink to that, he says. We go to the Officers Club and do just that.

Munda, New Georgia, April 21—Yesterday was my 26th birthday. After watching the movie *Princess O'Rourke* for the second time this month,

Pete and I proceeded to the Club for a small "surprise" celebration of the occasion. Drink followed drink until I was persuaded to demonstrate my specialty, the "Martha Graham Sit." I followed this with a couple of pirouettes, painfully learned by "spotting" on a doorknob in Martha's studio.

My performance was recorded for posterity by Russ, the bartender, in a cartoon-like watercolor, tonight on display behind the bar. It shows me in a tangle of twisted legs at the conclusion of a "triumphant" pirouette. Cheering, drunken flyers hover nearby.

Pete and I concluded the evening back at the tent, finishing the dregs of our hoarded "mission" whiskey, while I told him how I had learned to do vertical pirouettes in a Stearman biplane by spotting on a tobacco barn in a field far below. The instructor called it a "precision spin."

ADMIRALTY ISLANDS

The decision not to invade "Fortress Rabaul" was as surprising to allied troops as confounding to Japanese commanders. By-passing this greatest and most feared enemy base in the South Pacific was made possible by our taking the Admiralty Islands on February 29, 1944, some 400 miles northwest of Rabaul. The Bismarck Sea then became, in General Mac-Arthur's view, an allied "lake," and his relentless drive towards the Philippines intensified.

The US 1st Cavalry Division went ashore on the southeast coast of Los Negros, second largest island in the Admiralty group. It was the Cavalrymen's first combat assignment. General MacArthur watched their "baptism by fire" from the rail of the Cruiser "Phoenix." The landing was two months ahead of schedule and virtually unopposed. Momote Airfield, weed-covered and bomb-cratered, was taken within five hours. The real prize captured was 20-mile long, fleet-sized Seeadler Harbor, which separated Los Negros from Manus, largest island in the group, site of Margaret Mead's 1933 seminal study of primitive culture, *Growing up in New Guinea*.

Cost of the assault in American lives was a third of the 1,000-man invading force. 3,000 Japanese died. By-passed Rabaul was now doomed to wither and die. Its military commanders' greatest concern would be feeding the more than 100,000 Japanese troops and laborers stranded there.

Los Negros, Admiralty Islands, May 3—This has been "home" for only a few days but I already feel it may be the South Pacific island I dreamed of one day finding: a long, narrow, palm tree-covered finger of land which gently curves to the northwest, partially surrounding a 20-mile long natural harbor called Seeadler, its eastern shore an endless ribbon of gray-white sand facing the sea.

Our squadron's tents will be pitched on a slight rise overlooking this beach. We will face east, where our real home awaits us. Coconut palms guard the embankment. The surf, sometimes thunderous and threatening, is quiet and gentle at night. The steady on-shore breeze will keep us mosquito-free and cool. Rustling palm fronds, the soft hissing of shifting sands beneath the unfurling sheets of foam-speckled water, will lull us to sleep.

I use the future tense because our own tent still has not arrived from Munda, and we are sleeping in an unfinished mess hall beyond sight and sound of the sea.

Pete and I lingered at the beach until dark last night. He talked about the Pacific Ocean he remembered from nights spent at Kaleloch Beach on the northwestern coast of Washington. I described the Atlantic Ocean I saw at Jones Beach, trying to imagine how it would have looked without people.

Each of these moves by Group takes me farther and farther from those I love but it's the only direction I can go to find my way back.

Los Negros, Admiralty Islands, May 6—My first strike from this base— four days after arriving—was today's nine hour roundtrip flight to the Western Carolines, there to find and bomb a tiny atoll known as Woleai. There were a half-dozen atolls in the neighborhood, all looking like floating amoebas from 20,000 feet. Pete pointed to one and nodded. When it shot at us we knew he had found Woleai.

Woleai is arguably a target for two dozen B-24's because, says Intelligence, it's an important communications link in the air-sea route between Japanese naval bases at Palau, in the western Pacific, and our old friend, Truk, 1200 miles to the east. It has no airfield, only anti-aircraft guns to distinguish it from the neighbors. Today may have been the first time the guns were fired in anger, so far off-target were the rounds. The nearest airstrip is on Ulithi, 300 miles farther on. We did not wait around for Ulithian Zeros to greet us.

* * *

It's the return flight of these long missions that threatens one's sanity. The fear of a mechanical breakdown so many hours and miles from a landfall is constant, especially in a plane as old as "Frenisi." (Pete reminded me before takeoff that this is "Frenisi's" 71st combat mission!) The most trivial problem could eventually become a life-threatening situation. The many hours are thus spent checking all the gauges, one by one, again and again, for the slightest abnormal reading; and listening for any change in the drone of the four engines. All the while, one stares out at the vast, barren, blue-green sea, aching for the sight of a ship, even some floating debris, to dissemble the monochrome seascape. I was rewarded one time this afternoon by the brief, mirage-like appearance of a lone frigate bird, slowly skimming the surface far below. Whence did it come? Whither does it go?

I say it is the return flight I most fear, even though when outward bound we are more certain to confront disaster. But knowing even this provides some armor, enough knowledge and determination and strength to meet the known enemy. Returning, having survived the crucial encounter, one faces the unknown, and is never prepared or ready to do battle with this adversary.

So went my thoughts as I sometimes dozed, other times merely closed my eyes to the here and now, while Murphy minded the plane. The two of us seldom talk on these long flights, unless it's to discuss the plane or the mission. On the other hand, while I'm on duty, so to speak, and Murphy rests, Pete sometimes comes forward to keep me company. He squats in the narrow aisle between the pilots' seats, and we talk about various things having nothing whatsover to do with airplanes or missions. This afternoon he got started again on Faulkner, specifically *Absalom, Absalom!*, which he recently acquired. I have not read it and mostly just listened to Pete explain the biblical allusions. Later, I told him about my somewhat unsettling meeting last night with Sam and Gino, whom I have not seen since we arrived out here last November and went our separate ways.

"Sam's the one who dated James Hilton's secretary or whatever, right?" "Once," I remind him. "Gino's got the uncle with mob connections, right?" "Wrong!" I say. "Uncle just promised to take care of him after the war."

I was in the Mess Hall, drinking coffee and watching some guys play poker, when I heard my name called. I looked up to see Gino and Sam standing there. They had learned I was in the 307th Group and decided to pay a visit. They're both in the 5th Group, based at Momote Field, only a few miles from our camp here at Mokerang. The two Groups usually join forces on missions, and I expect Sam and Gino also flew to Woleai today. I was somewhat relieved to learn both are still co-pilots.

We talked mostly about missions and Auckland. We were on rest leave at different times, but found the same night clubs and pubs and restaurants. I did not mention having seen Frankie, whom both had briefly met. Nor did I remind Sam of the time, last December, when we saw one another at Koli Beach and simply waved, neither of us stopping, merely saying "Hi!" and walking on in opposite directions.

Before Sam and Gino left we tried to account for the other fellows who came overseas with us on Eleanor Roosevelt's C-87. We could confirm that six have been shot down in combat, one sent home after a mental breakdown. That leaves six unaccounted for; and Sam, Gino and me.

"Count your blessings," said Pete. We stared at the sea in silence for a few minutes, then Pete went back to his charts. "Mokerang by 2:00 PM," he announced a few minutes later.

I thought about Sam and Gino for the rest of the trip back to Mokerang. Sam had the same unease on his face last night as the time we passed one another on the beach without talking. His blue-gray eyes no longer twinkle as he talks, seem always averted, darting here and there at every unexpected sound or movement. Gino was less changed, his face still suddenly wrinkling as if with the memory of a smile. His dark, glistening eyes would still fix on mine to hold my attention while he spoke. But last night there was a trace of a smile on his face even as he told about his pilot taking some flak in the throat, and of the time the plane flying off his wing suddenly blew up . . .

The truck taking us back to camp from the airfield after the mission overtook a trickling file of natives walking along the edge of the road. They looked alike from the rear, all wearing long colored skirts, nothing above the waist. As we passed by I could see that some were men, some were women, and that several of the women were pregnant and had shaved heads. Pete said these had been raped by Japanese soldiers; their children, when born, would be killed.

Los Negros, Admiralty Islands, May 8—Today's mission took us 750 miles due west to one of the Schouten Islands, Biak, where we bombed Mokmer Airdrome. Dozens of Zekes on the ground but only three came up and did not attack. We suspect they were there to get our course and altitude for the anti-aircraft gunners down below. Is this why the A-A was so accurate? Heavy, too. Several of our planes were hit, but not "Frenisi."

One plane from the 424th squadron was so shot up it did not make it back to Los Negros. I monitored its brief, unsettling radio conversation with another B-24 flying nearby. Best I can remember, the dialogue went something like this, punctuated by long silences:

"What casualties?"

"None."

"Damage?"

"Two engines. #3 is feathered. #1 running wild; can't feather it. #2 is overheating and #4 is losing oil. Losing altitude like mad."

"Bomber Command says a Dumbo is looking for you. If you ditch, he'll be there."

"Hope so!"

"My tail section's all shot up. Rudder no good. Still losing altitude. Down to five-thousand feet already."

"That's Owi Island off your left wing. Japs there."

"Roger. Crew's dumping everything loose. Chopping out the rest."

"#2 just cut out. Giving order to jump when we hit 1500 feet."

"Good luck, buddy!"

"Bailing out!"

Learned later, at de-briefing, that all but one of the plane's crew members got picked up by a Navy "Dumbo," one of those two-engine PBY Catalina "Flying Boats" that skim the seas after each mission to rescue survivors of planes shot down by the Japanese. One guy was seen jumping before the others, apparently before the pilot's order to jump was given. No one saw him in the water. Possibly his 'chute didn't open; or a Japanese sub cruising off Owi Island might have snatched him.

Los Negros, Admiralty Islands, May 10—We're now "at home" in our new "Tree House," so called because the platform of our tent is atop the trunk and roots of a tremendous tree growing out of an embankment at the edge of the beach. The section of the tree, with its tangle of leaf-covered branches, that extends beyond the platform, is over the surf in which we swim.

The platform-floor is 7 to 8 feet above the ground, accessible by means of ladder-steps from the beach. We even have a cellar of our own: there's an abandoned half-hidden Japanese foxhole dug directly beneath us, with an entrance on either side of the tree, one leading to a slit trench. (Where deluded Nippon warriors watched MacArthur's 1st Cavalry troops stride ashore?) We have a startling view out over the ocean from each of our cots, and can luxuriate in cooling sea breezes at night.

The lumber for the platform and tent frame is "dunnage," the lumber used on "Liberty" ships to separate the layers of cargo in the hold. Pete, Murphy and I visited the Harbormaster for Seeadler Harbor on a tip that he could help us. He not only told us of a ship that had just unloaded and had "dunnage" to get rid of, he also provided us with one of those amphibious trucks we call "Ducks" to get the lumber. The only payment he wanted was a ride in a B-24, and we immediately agreed to take him aboard "Frenisi" the next time we took her up for a flight test.

Getting the lumber was simply a matter of driving—sailing? across the harbor in the Duck to the designated "Liberty" ship, watch the cargo net lower the lumber into our "truck," then drive—sail back across the bay. Our Duck driver took us directly up on the shore, to the nearest cross-island road, to our tent site.

We had a small house-warming party this afternoon, fueled by the last half-bottle of bourbon. Murphy had swiped an unlabled, flat tin of some kind of food from the mess hall. He hoped it might be paté. Pete guessed sardines. I thought tuna fish. It was corned beef. One of our "guests" had brought Ritz crackers, a treasured item out here, so we had a "party" after all.

After dinner (*fresh* meat—beef—for the first time since arriving here May 3), Pete, Murphy and I (Hunter seldom spends his free time with us; he has friends in another squadron) visited the Harbormaster in his tent to thank him more substantially for his help in getting the lumber. Again he said all he wanted was a ride in a B-24. We assured him that would happen, meantime invited him to share the brandy and rum we brought along. He did. And showed us some particularly graphic Japanese propaganda leaflets. The "cartoons" are professionally drawn, tastefully colored if somewhat explicit: one panel shows an American GI having intercourse with an Australian girl; the second is of an Australian soldier, in uniform, having a black, native girl "dog fashion." The caption, in English, advises the Australian to "take his time," warning that the American GI will take good care of the Aussie's girlfriend back home.

Despite the relative luxury of having a beach-front tent site, cooling breezes flowing through the tent at night, and an almost nightly view of the moon rising from the sea, squadron living conditions are not yet comparable to Guadalcanal or Munda. We do not have screening or electric lights in our tents. The exclusively canned and dehydrated food we eat is still indiscriminately ladled into our undivided mess kit dish which each of us must wash after the meal in a common tub of boiling water. There is no PX—but candy and cigarettes are free. Drinking water comes from canvas lister bags hung from trees, is always lukewarm, and slightly medicinal in taste. The nearest pit latrine is a half-mile from our tent, but "Pee-Tubes" are everywhere: an iron pipe pounded into the ground, a funnel stuck into the top of the pipe. The stench of urine at these locations is sometimes overwhelming. Until a laundry unit arrives, some of us tie our soiled clothes to the end of a long rope which we throw into the surf. After the clothes have rubbed along the sandy bottom a few days, we haul them out and hang them on a line, hopefully to be rinsed free of salt and sand by the daily rain showers. A half-hour exposure to the noonday sun takes care of the drying process. We wash and shave from steel helmets with tepid rain water caught in the tied-off tent flaps. Showers, when fresh water is available, are taken under large steel barrels resting on a high, overhead scaffold. Punctured beer cans serve as showerheads.

* * *

I completed six months of my South Pacific sentence today. The next mission I fly will be my 25th. I must be half-way home . . . please?

Los Negros, Admiralty Islands, May 15—We carried a new kind of bomb to Biak yesterday. Only the bombardiers knew beforehand that the 500 pounders were rigged with proximity fuses. They could be set to explode at a predetermined height *above* ground. Their purpose, of course, was to kill as many people as possible in the vicinity of the target. "Daisy Cutters" is what our bombardier called them. Hunter told us that we were carrying them after one of the planes blew up, in the air, shortly after takeoff.

The plane that blew up was from the 5th Group. Sam and Gino's outfit. The 5th Group planes alternated their takeoffs from Momote Field with our takeoffs from Mokerang Field. We rendezvoused over Seeadler Harbor.

I was at the controls of "Frenisi" when we took off yesterday morning. Murphy decided this at the very last minute so I had to fly from the co-pilot's seat, on the righthand side of the ship. Always awkward, holding the four throttle controls in the left hand. I had just started down the runway when I saw this plane in the air, on the left, low, overtaking me. Murphy said it was the plane I was supposed to follow. I kept "Frenisi" on the runway as long as possible, to give the other plane time to pull farther ahead—I was worried about his prop-wash. Finally, I ran out of runway and had to lift off.

We were closer to him than I wanted to be. His prop-wash hit us almost immediately. I needed both hands and both feet to keep us level. Soon as Murphy got the landing gear up, he grabbed the wheel, too.

I decided it was too rough staying this close behind him. I had just begun easing us over to the left when that plane I was following, just blew up! Smoke, flames, debris right there in front of us. Murphy and I instinctively put "Frenisi" into a steep, banking turn to the left, and kept turning. By the time we came back full-circle, I could see chunks of the fuselage and pieces of the tail section floating on the water.

The tower immediately directed us to proceed on to Biak as planned. As if nothing had happened. It was then Hunter told us about the special bombs we were carrying. He said they were supposedly set to explode at fifty feet above ground. Those that blew up the plane were set wrong or simply malfunctioned. The plane was up at least a thousand feet by then. But the fatal mistake, of course, was arming the bombs before takeoff. That should not have been done until later, at altitude. Hunter assured us that our bombs were not armed.

* * *

We hit Biak's Mokmer Airdrome with our special bombs. The revetment areas alongside the runway. Went right where Hunter wanted them to go. Cut all the daisies in sight, he said.

When we got to debriefing, back on Los Negros, I asked Ben to find out who was flying the plane that blew up. Were either Sam or Gino aboard? He did not have an answer for me until evening. We were all down on the beach when he came by the tent. An officer from the Merchant Marine ship that gave us the lumber for our tent platform had brought us a case of fresh eggs. We fried and scrambled three dozen on pans borrowed from the mess hall. The "stove" was a five-gallon tin filled with sand soaked in 100-octane gasoline. We had invited our ground crew over to share the feast. And now Ben. He was able to confirm that neither Sam nor Gino were on the plane that blew up.

Los Negros, Admiralty Islands, May 17—Saw the face of the enemy for the first time today. Prisoners of war, I hasten to add. Japs. Remembered reading of a *Time* editor telling his writers, the day after Pearl Harbor, "Now you can call them Japs."

Pete and I came upon the POW stockade by accident. We had jeeped over to the little village of Lorengau, on Manus island, hoping to see some of the places Margaret Mead described in her book *Growing Up In New Guinea*. It was really about Manus, not New Guinea. Anyway, the MP's we asked for directions said the whole island, except for Lorengau, was off-limits. Japs still running around loose. The ones the Cavalrymen captured alive were in the stockade down the road, if we wanted to take a look.

Those we saw in the stockade were small, emaciated, expressionless men, wearing only a loincloth. They stared straight ahead, avoided our eyes, clung to the wire fencing of the cage-like affair. They were confined and displayed like animals in a zoo.

The MPs on guard had rifles hanging loose from one shoulder, more concerned about revengeful, trigger-happy Cavalrymen than the possibility these pathetic creatures might attempt to escape.

On the drive back to Los Negros I tell Pete about the Japanese I had met before the war: S. I. Hayakawa, professor of linguistics at the University of Wisconsin; ballet dancer Sono Osato and her sister, Teru; and Isamu Noguchi, designer of stage sets for Martha Graham.

"Not Japs," said Pete.

Los Negros, Admiralty Islands, May 18—Today's strike, once again over Biak's sun-scorched cliffs and limestone terraces—a moonscape from 20-thousand feet—but this time not to the cluster of airfields, our usual target. Today we aimed our bombs at nearby Bosnek Town, on the shores of Japen Sea, seeking out anti-aircraft batteries said to be hidden among the residents' gardens and thatched-roof houses. Only on one previous mission—to Rabaul Town—have we dropped bombs on civilians. Those we dropped today were not, I was relieved to learn, the infamous "Daisy-Cutters" of previous missions.

The bomb run was uneventful. Why we were not pursued by the many Zeros we saw tethered on the ground at nearby Mokmer Airdrome, no one could understand.

On the return flight to Los Negros, Pete, as usual, kept watch with me while Murphy slept. We were rewarded this trip by being able to hear the short-wave broadcast of a symphony concert in Australia. It lasted for hours, all the while we flew on and on, through a brilliant blue sky, skirting the occasional towering snow-white clouds, and watching with amazement the formation of rainbows in complete circles, some even surrounding the plane, others forming a ring around a cloud. Remnants of torn clouds brushed the windscreen with an iridescent froth that sparkled in the mid-afternoon sun. Tiny, whitecap dots speckled the blue-green sea below . . .

It was hours later when I finally saw the towering, castle-like cloud on the horizon I knew guarded Los Negros. Then I could discern the island itself, a thin pencil line drawn at the bottom of the sky. I switched the radio to Mokerang Tower's frequency to await instructions as we began our measured descent to a lower, more friendly altitude that did not require oxygen masks. Other planes from the squadron were now appearing, all unseen since leaving Biak—except one we caught dumping its bombs that for some unknown reason were not dropped on the target. The tower began giving landing instructions: altimeter setting, wind direction and velocity, and so on. The squadron leader interrupted to tell us to close in for a coordinated landing.

We were now in stepped-down tandem flights of three planes, thundering towards that hovering cloud. I thought of us as twelve straining, exhausted flying horses nearing the finish line. When the lead plane reached the island's off-shore coral reefs, we saw it rock its wings, the signal to begin our peal-off: a shallow dive, then the pull-up into a steep, climbing turn to the left. I drop the landing gear. We are now ready to leave the sky. As we begin the swift descent, Murphy aims "Frenisi" at the center of the strip below. Tex calls air speed; I lower flaps; Murphy increases the RPMs. I feel the jar of the touch-down, hear the squeal of the tires on the steel matting.

Murphy holds the nose wheel high as we hurtle towards the end of the runway. I glimpse the clutch of crew chiefs leaning against a fire truck, always there to see if their own plane made it back. Now Murphy eases the nose wheel down and the two of us begin stomping the brakes. Windows are slid open and the flight deck is flooded with warm, sea-fresh air. Headsets and helmets are flung aside, belts and straps unbuckled. I fill out the Flight Report as we taxi back to the hardstand where our crew chief, Kurt, awaits us.

* * *

A little later, at de-briefing, I struggle to find words to describe what I saw and did and felt. I search the maps for the remembered tiny, angry red flashes of gunbursts four miles below our plane. I do not mention the symphony concert I attended or the display of circular rainbows I witnessed. But on the slow walk back to the tent, I think about those little gardens and thatched-roof houses in Bosnek that today were shadowed by the wings of our airplanes.

From the perch of our tent platform, I can see again the towering castle cloud, hovering still, on guard at this sanctuary.

Los Negros, Admiralty Islands, May 20—While censoring enlisted men's mail this morning, a voluntary duty all officers are invited to perform, I drew a letter addressed to Robert Casadesus, presumably the well-known French pianist. The mailing address was Montreal, Canada. There was no clue as to the nature of the relationship, and no mention of music. The newly arrived corporal merely described the daily routine during his first few weeks on this "most tropical of islands."

* * *

Murphy and I spent about 30-minutes in the air today checking one of "Frenisi's" engines for the crew chief. We took along as passengers the three officers of the Liberty ship from which we got the lumber for our tent platform, and the Harbor Master who supplied the "Duck" used to transport the boards. We let each of the men take a turn "piloting" from my co-pilot's seat. After the flight, Murphy and I were invited to join them for lunch aboard their ship. We dined on Manhattan clam chowder, roast beef, fresh potatoes, homemade bread, real butter, iced lemonade, strong American-style coffee, and vanilla ice cream. What a feast!

* * *

One more disease has been added to our "worry" list—Scrub Typhus. It's transmitted by the bite of a tiny mite found in tall grass hereabout. Those stricken experience a very high fever which, we are warned, can be fatal or cause permanent damage to the eyes, brain, or both. We were ordered to soak all our outer clothing in large vats of a liquid chemical. And to stay out of tall grass. The "worry" list already includes malaria, dengue fever, yellow fever, and elephantiasis. And homesickness.

Los Negros, Admiralty Islands, May 24—Large package from Franny today containing all twelve volumes of Dorothy Richardson's novel *Pilgrimage*. Don't know Richardson's work but remember reading somewhere that she employs a technique called "interior monologue," presumably similar to James Joyce's "stream of consciousness." Hopefully, Richardson will be less demanding. I send money to Franny from time to time to buy books she thinks might interest me. The small library of donated books we have out here is limited mostly to "popular" novels, although I did find Proust's *Swann's Way* there.

* * *

General MacArthur's Headquarters today announced last week's capture of Wakde Island. None of us had ever heard of it. Pete finally found it on one of his charts, off the coast of Dutch New Guinea, 100 miles north of Hollandia, MacArthur's headquarters since April.

* * *

The correspondence between the corporal and Casadesus continues. The corporal writes that he has asked permission to visit a native village on Manus. I had to cut out the word "Manus," of course. Said he wants to investigate a claim he read in some book that the Manus natives have no real music tradition and cannot even carry a tune. I tell Ben about the correspondence. He is intrigued. Says an uncle of his, a painter, has a large studio on East 72nd Street in New York. It has two concert grand pianos in it and Ben says his uncle has occasionally had Walter Damrosch over to play two-piano duets with him. Ben is positive his uncle mentioned Casadesus visiting the studio.

Los Negros, Admiralty Islands, May 27—US 41st Division troops today invaded Biak, presumably putting an end to our non-stop raids on that desolate island. We were there to hit Jap beach defenses before the troops went ashore. I was co-piloting "Frenisi" for Dick Gilbert, recently named Operations Officer of the squadron, and lead pilot of this multi-group mission. Our Flight Surgeon came along for the ride, hopeful it might be a "medal" mission. Double the whisky ration for the strike, we told him, and we'll guarantee a medal. He smiled.

It was a successful mission, if not worthy of a medal, but unusual for two reasons: while circling at the rendezvous coordinates, waiting for Fifth Air Force planes to join us, we suddenly came under attack by anti-aircraft guns. We were far off-shore from Biak, and knew it could not be coming from there. Then, looking down through the clouds, we saw ships of the US Navy. They were there to do pre-invasion shelling of the beaches, not shoot down B-24s.

Gilbert and I suddenly remembered we had been instructed to turn off our IFF radar detection device for the mission. Someone in Bomber Command thought this would confuse Jap aircraft. It did not confuse the US Navy. With the device turned off, we were a "Foe" to them, not a "Friend." I quickly turned the IFF switch back on, and Gilbert advised all the other planes to do the same. The Navy stopped shooting at us.

We had another, less life-threatening problem this morning. About the time we began dodging Navy anti-aircraft fire, first the tail gunner, then a waist gunner, and finally most every member of the crew, called up on the intercom to ask permission to go to the bomb-bay and open the doors. All were suffering from diarrhea. After the IFF problem was solved, even Gilbert excused himself. For several minutes, the Flight Surgeon and I were quite alone on the flight deck—no pilot, no navigator, no flight engineer. The Doc wondered if this made it a "medal" mission. I told him to wait and see what happened next.

It was all anti-climax from then on. The Navy shelled, we bombed, the troops went ashore. But a happy surprise when we got back to Los Negros: the roster of names for Rest Leave in Sydney, Australia, was posted. My name was there, at the bottom of the list where the "Zs" usually are. I'm off in two days.

Los Negros, Admiralty Islands, May 31—Hank Walters, onetime cadet roommate, almost best man, erstwhile FBI spotter, is a prisoner of war in Germany. His B-17 was shot down January 17. He bailed out but was captured and now languishes at Stalag I on the Baltic coast.

I am so informed by his wife, Roberta. The last letter I sent to him at his base in England was forwarded to her. She hopes I will write to him but cautions I must not reveal my military status or mention my current address. She warns all letters to him are rigorously censored.

I associate all the joys and thrills—and fears—of learning to fly with Hank. Roberta's bitter-sweet letter recounted some of those deliriously exciting and happy experiences he had shared with her.

* * *

Another flood of memories was spilled by a letter from Martha, also in today's mail. She told of a week of concerts in New York by her Company during which she revived some of the old works, including the solo, *Frontier*, which she had not done in five years and said now belongs to the public, not to her.

Letter To The World was also given, and during its performance, Martha wrote,

> ". . . you were so strongly in my thoughts that I spoke of you to Jean. We were standing ready to go on after the Party scene. I had the certainty that I saw your feet dancing in the dance."

And, of course, I thought of the last time I did dance in *Letter*, the night we gave the special performance for Benoit-Levy, on the eve of my joining the Air Force . . .

Tomorrow, I fly to Australia for the long awaited rest leave. The remains of tonight will be spent disassembling memories of that other world Martha's letter brought back to life. And dreaming of Sydney.

* * *

Kings Cross, Sydney, NSW, June 3—Twenty-four hundred miles are now wedged between me and the Admiralty Islands. Forgotten for a time are the unquiet nights, stifling days, wasting rains, and the fated pre-dawn missions. I have once again stepped through the looking glass into a never-never land, like Auckland, where one sleeps in dreams and jousts only with small honking cars and bell-ringing bicycles speeding along the "wrong" side of the street; and where the days are cooled by breezes, not tropical downpours.

I've been here only three days but already remember to return the salute of enlisted men, and to touch the visor of my uniform cap when passing a lady. Re-learning the size and value of pence, shillings, florins and crowns will require more time.

I write this in a room rented from a Mrs. Clark whose house is in King's Cross, Sydney's "Greenwich Village." I much prefer this arrangement to staying at a downtown military-operated hotel as I did in Auckland. I'm using the room formerly occupied by Mrs. Clark's son, now an officer in the Australian Army's legal affairs section. His passion is music, not law, she says. A Bechstein piano and the large record collection in the parlor convince me. My room is upstairs, on what Mrs. Clark calls the First Floor, which I think is the Second Floor. Rent is three pounds a week, about $10.

Mrs. Clark has invited me to tea. Later, I plan to join Dick Gilbert and others at the "Lord Nelson" on Kent Street for something stronger. Dinner elsewhere will follow, preceded by a dozen or so Rock oysters.

Sydney, NSW, June 7—I heard about D-Day last night in a King's Cross night club while dancing with an Aussie Red Cross gal I had just met. The band abruptly stopped playing; a man strode across the dance floor to the microphone by the piano and announced that Allied troops had landed on the coast of Normandy. Everyone applauded. Someone shouted "Good show!" Those of us on the dance floor stood where we were as if waiting to be told what to do next. People talked in hushed voices. One could hear the sound of chairs being moved, the tinkle of glasses being tapped. My dance partner excused herself and went back to the table. Dick Gilbert came over to where I was standing. "Christ-all-mighty!" was all he said. We shook hands, not knowing what else to do. The band began playing *God Save the King*. Dick and I hurried back to the table. Everyone was standing and applauding. Then the band struggled through *The Star Spangled Banner*. It sounded like a dirge. People kept applauding. I heard a few whistles. We ordered another round of drinks.

Sydney, NSW, June 9—This is the final day of my leave, the last chance I'll have to indulge my new-found passion for rock oysters and king prawns; and, of course, my unquenchable thirst for the dark, bitter Australian beer—even if always warm. It's been a week devoted, if unseemly, to an endless succession of lunches and dinners and pub "crawls."

My companions—mostly guys from the squadron—share my appetite for the food and beer. It's the seafood I crave, but steak-and-eggs, as in Auckland, is possibly the most popular dish.

I'm intrigued by the Aussies, so unlike the New Zealanders—quite mad by comparison: pleasantly, joyously mad. Their shared smiles are infectious, their laughter intoxicating. But here, as when flying, I'm ever the spectator, merely an observer of these happy people in their fun and games.

I've had only the one date since coming here, the night D-Day was announced, with the Red Cross gal. The other nights, Dick Gilbert and I searched for new restaurants and nightclubs with small bands that Dick invariably joined at the piano before closing time.

But tonight, on my last night, I have a "blind" date with the daughter of my landlady's best friend. The girl is a university student in Melbourne and returns home to Sydney on weekends. I should know better, but the gal's name is "Dymphna." How could I not want to meet her?

Sydney, NSW, June 10—Dick and I taxied to the airfield in silence, resigned to settling for so brief a visit to this Aussie paradise. It was not yet 6:00 AM when we arrived at the field and joined the line of airmen, silently and very slowly, shuffling towards a waiting C-47 parked at the edge of the apron. Its starboard engine was already started. Like most of the others in line, my shuffle was slowed by an over-stuffed B-4 bag—mine weighed down by many well-wrapped bottles of Scotch. I had dreams that genie-like memories of the past week would be released from them in days to come.

My reverie was suddenly interrupted by a C-47 crew member yelling at us to go back to Operations, that the plane was full. I watched in amazement as he slammed the door shut, the #2 engine started up, and the plane began to taxi away. Operations told us to go back to Headquarters in Sydney and sign up for the next flight, which we learned to our delight was a week from today!

* * *

I'm now back at Mrs. Clark's house, listening for the tinkle of her little silver bell that will tell me tea is ready. I went back to bed immediately after returning from Headquarters, am now refreshed and ready to resume the Sydney routine. I'll pay Mrs. Clark the rent for another week, then tell her about my date with her friend's daughter. I very much hope to see Dymphna again.

Tonight at the King's Arms, Dick and I will celebrate our great good fortune of learning the secret of extending one's leave: arrive late at the airfield, and stay at the end of the line to the plane!

Sydney, NSW, June 11—For the second successive Sunday I have been awakened by church bells, not a basketball whistle telling me it is time to get dressed for a mission. I have no difficulty adjusting to the sound of church bells. Already, after just a week, I feel very much at home. Driving on the "wrong" side seems perfectly normal. I have no difficulty adding and subtracting pence, shillings and pounds—at my own pace.

Sydney is a charming, "old world" city like Auckland, but larger, busier and more cosmopolitan. I especially like the older downtown sections, with their narrow, winding streets. All public buildings are of a grand scale, most built of sandstone. The two cathedrals, one Anglican, the other Catholic, are huge, magnificent structures. I visited both during the week.

Most spectacular sight of all is the beautiful land-locked harbor. The city rises along its shores. The bay is spanned by the highest, longest suspension bridge I have ever seen.

I am constantly reminded of New York City. Streets and sidewalks are always crowded. The air is filled with sounds of car horns—and trolley bells, here. King's Cross has more private residences than Greenwich Village but its many small shops, night clubs, bookstores, alleys, and twisting, narrow streets, remind me of my former home.

But what makes Sydney truly unique are the many beautiful parks and public gardens scattered throughout the city. And its spectacular harbor.

Sydney, NSW, June 21—My address is still King's Cross, Sydney. Last Saturday, the 17th, Dick and I succeeded in extending our rest leave one more week by the simple, obvious ruse of arriving late at the airfield. The plane was fully loaded before our turn to board came. There is only one flight to Los Negros each week.

My happiness is tainted with guilt. My penance was to forgo the "Lord Nelson" in favor of spending several evenings with Mrs. Clark. On one occasion she permitted me to use the Bechstein to play my three-piece repertoire of excerpts from "Rhapsody in Blue," "Clair de Lune," and "Zing! Went The Strings of My Heart." The Bechstein sounded fine but it did not improve my memory or technique. Or taste in composers, said Mrs. Clark, who followed my performance with several recordings of Mozart concerti.

Sydney, NSW, June 22—I have seen Dymphna twice since our first date, both times in the afternoon. Night clubs and movies do not interest her. Last week we visited the Royal Botanical Gardens; today we walked the streets of Hunters Hill, an historical section of the city originally settled by wealthy French immigrants, whose old stone houses are the chief attraction. There's a spectacular view of Sydney's skyline from here.

We do not talk about the war. The first time we met she told me that her father had been killed on the Kokoda Trail by a Japanese sniper while ministering to some wounded soldiers. He was a doctor and had been drafted into service. She never again mentioned the war. She knows I am a flyer because of my pilot's wings but does not question me about combat. She is interested in the sensation of flying, however, and wonders how the earth looks from great heights, whether I have ever seen a bird up there, what the inside of a cloud looks like, and if the sun is shining above an overcast. She has read all of St. Exupery's books.

Most of Dymphna's questions concern New York City. She seems obsessed by the place and is determined to visit it after the war. Her ambition is to be a writer. She was very surprised to learn I had been a dancer but did not know what "modern" dance was. I attempted to explain how it differs from ballet. She wondered if I will go back to dancing after the war. I said I did not think so.

I do not expect to see Dymphna again. I return to Los Negros day after tomorrow. I told her I hoped she would come to New York after the war. She said she would bring me a copy of her first novel if she came.

Sydney, NSW, June 23—At tea today, Mrs. Clark told me about her life before the war, when she and her husband lived in London, then Paris; and of how he lost all their money on ill-advised investments, including some in German enterprises, soon after which he unexpectedly died. Mrs. Clark and her then teenage son, and the Bechstein piano, returned to Sydney to live on the small inheritance she could collect only by re-establishing residence in Australia.

It did not seem a sad story as Mrs. Clark told it. There was no bitterness in her voice, only regret that her husband did not live to fight the Nazis. And the Japanese.

Earlier today, Dick and I found our way to a well-known department store called "David Jones" to look for something to take back to Los Negros. I ended up with a "shooting stick," so-called, a walking stick or cane with a handle that opens up into a seat. I figured it would be useful to sit on in a pub or officers club while "hunting" for a stool at the bar.

Brisbane, June 25—Dick and I made sure we were on today's flight out of Sydney, but three hours later our C-47 was back on the ground, still in Australia, having lost one of its engines and forced to make an emergency landing at an abandoned Aussie fighter airstrip.

We had just flown past Brisbane, on our way north to Townsville, when one of the two engines began throwing oil and spluttering and had to be shut off. The pilot looked in vain for a smooth beach for a wheels-up landing, then called Amberly Airfield, outside Brisbane, for help. They gave him directions to the fighter airstrip, located a few miles inland from an unpronounceable coastal town named Maroochydore.

On the way inland from Maroochydore, the plane's one engine had difficulty maintaining altitude so the pilot ordered us to throw overboard all our luggage. Out went my B-4 bag and the Johnnie Walker Red scotch, but not my shooting stick.

The pilot quickly found the airstrip, brought us straight in, just above the trees, to a ker-plunk landing beside the Aussie CO and his half-dozen caretaker-airmen. He invited us to lunch in a corner of their squadron-sized mess hall. We dined on Spam sandwiches and lukewarm tea from tin cups.

The CO then volunteered his men to help search for the luggage we had thrown from the plane. The pilot remembered our compass heading from Maroochydore to the field, so we set off in a couple of lorries to begin a search of the bush. We soon came upon a farmer who said he saw our low-flying plane coming from the east with only one propeller turning and disgorging bags and things down into his field of sugar beets and the bush beyond. We formed a flying-wedge of men and began scouring the countryside with the compass-carrying Aussie CO in the lead.

By dusk we had found only a couple of the B-4 bags. Not mine. We were then taken by bus back to Brisbane and installed in the Hotel Albert. The search is to continue in the morning while a maintenance crew from Amberley attempts to repair the failed engine.

Brisbane, June 28—This unexpected layover in Brisbane goes on and on. Adding to our unease at seeming to have deserted our comrades on Los Negros, today we were informed that the malfunctioning engine cannot be repaired locally. Another C-47 will have to be sent to pick us up. Possibly by the end of the week.

Spent the past two days in the "bush," as the countryside here is called, searching for the luggage we kicked out of the plane. With the help of the Aussie airmen, we found all but three of the 20-odd bags. Mine reeked unashamedly of whisky given up by the broken bottles. The drenched clothing had also been shredded by the shards of glass. Dick's gear smelled strongly of gin.

Brisbane is only half the size of Sydney and seems very provincial by comparison. There is a university, however, and a large art museum, in addition to the obligatory Catholic and Protestant cathedrals. I have visited none of these "sights" to date.

General MacArthur maintains his headquarters down the street at the Lennon Hotel. Ours is maintained at the Albert. Residents of the twain have not met.

En Route to Los Negros, July 1—Finally departed Brisbane late yesterday afternoon and flew north along the Queensland coast to Townsville where we spent the night. On arrival, coming in over the bay, and the harbor crowded with docks and piers and cargo ships, I watched a blood-red sun slide down behind thousand-foot high Castle Hill which guards this little frontier town.

This morning, the same blood-red sun rose from the Coral Sea as we took off and briefly flew into its glare to gain altitude before heading north. The Barrier Reef was dimly visible in the shadowy waters far below. A thousand miles beyond the horizon, in the Bismark Sea, Los Negros awaits. There I will tether my Sydney memories of green lawns and crowded sidewalks, clanging trolleys and tinkling bicycle bells, the secret smiles and quiet laughter, to nourish my loneliness until all this ends.

* * *

Los Negros, Admiralty Islands, July 2—How easily one adjusts to an un-forgiving sun, enfeebling humidity, shrieking gulls, and the whines of protesting airplane engines. Off-shore breezes are scented with urine from Pee-Tubes, not the remembered perfume of pretty girls hurrying to catch a tram. . . .

But it's "home" of a kind and I'm happy to be back. On waking this morning, I instinctively glance over to the cot opposite mine. It's late morning—I've slept dreamless the whole night through—and, of course, Pete is not there, arms crossed over his chest, a cigarette between his lips; but neither is Hans, his replacement, who could have slept in, with today's mission cancelled. But the empty cot is made up, drum-tight, mosquito net neatly tied back. Pete would have skipped the housekeeping in favor of just lying about on so rare a free day. I hope Hans is as good a navigator as bed-maker.

51 letters arrived during the month of my absence. I found them on my return yesterday afternoon all neatly sorted and stacked by return address (Hans?). One was from Pete, now home in Seattle. He tells of his last mission in "Frenisi," her 93rd. He did not say what number it was for him. I think he stopped counting after Truk.

Pete left a good part of himself here in the South Pacific. He does not write about being home, only of what happened out here. The letter details the story of W., a co-pilot who joined our squadron shortly before I went to Sydney. W. came overseas about the time Pete did, more than a year ago. His plane was shot down off Choiseul early on—his second or third mission. Only he and the bombardier, R., survived, rescued by natives, who eventually got them back to Guadalcanal in outrigger canoes. Both refused to fly combat after that experience and were promptly relegated to demeaning ground jobs. W. supervised the refueling of transient aircraft. Last month, after almost a year in that purgatory, W. pleaded to be put back on flying status. He told Pete it was the only way he'd ever get home. Pete warned him that flying again might render him too dead to go home. W. said he'd take his chances.

End of story as Pete told it in the letter: W. got assigned to a crew soon after I left for Sydney. On the day of W.'s first mission, Pete was in the S-2 tent, waiting for the planes to return. When W.'s crew came in for de-briefing, W. was not with them. The pilot said their plane was jumped by a Zeke during the bomb run; a 20mm shell caught W. straight on. He was the only casualty.

Pete said that later the same day he ran into R., the bombardier who had also refused to fly after the Choiseul thing. He told Pete he had heard

W. was flying again, wondered how it was going, that he was thinking of asking to go back on flying status, too. Pete said he had to tell him what happened to W. Pete said he heard later that R. decided to stay on the ground.

Los Negros, Admiralty Islands, July 3—Today's mission, my first since the end of May, was also the longest one I've ever flown—13 hours and 10 minutes. We flew to Yap, in the Western Carolines, to hit its airfield.

The mission was special for another reason: it was to be "Frenisi's" 100th and, presumably, last. She had been assigned to another crew while I was in Sydney, I was sorry to learn, so I did not get to fly her. In fact, I did not even see her during the mission.

As it turned out, the airfield we were supposed to hit was hidden by clouds, and we had to salvo the bombs and merely hope they did some damage. At that moment, we were much more concerned with some 16 Jap fighter planes that suddenly appeared overhead. They stayed with us for nearly 45 minutes but did no serious damage to any of our planes. Even lobbed a couple of air-burst phosphorus bombs into the formation to no avail. Our gunners did no better and did not claim any kills.

Tonight, after the movie, those of us who at one time or another had flown "Frenisi" met at the Club to toast the old lady. We all agreed she should be spared the indignity of a War Bond tour back in the States. Better that she end up being bull-dozed off the end of a runway, into the sea.

Twenty-six of my 30 missions to date were flown in "Frenisi." Of all those present at the Club tonight, only Murphy could top that number. This almost, but not quite, makes me an "old timer."

Los Negros, Admiralty Islands, July 5—The takeoff was before midnight on today's strike to Yap, the plan being to smash the Japs' planes on the ground before breakfast. So much for well-laid plans. Only eight of our 12 planes found Sorol Islands, the designated rendezvous, 150 miles this side of Yap. Our squadron leader did not. We circled and circled, vainly waiting for him to show up, wasting precious fuel and time, until learning he had long since turned back with an engine out. By the time another leader was designated, the sun was up, the Japs had eaten their breakfast, and 28 of their fighters were in the air waiting for us.

Our substitute leader's plane got so shot up over the target that he radioed in the clear that he was going to try for a water landing. This proved impossible, the plane was so badly damaged. I counted only five parachutes in the air before the plane hit the water. Saw no rafts or parachutes when we circled the area but heard on the radio that a "Dumbo" PBY was on its way to search.

Another of our planes, I learned later, was so badly damaged that when it got back to Mokerang Field, only the left landing gear could be lowered. The pilot gave the crew members the option of jumping or staying aboard for a wheels-up landing. He had to bring the plane in: the bombardier had accidently lost his parachute harness out the bomb bay and could not jump.

Six men bailed out, three of whom were injured in the jump. Hans Meier, who lives in our tent, and is usually our navigator, was aboard that plane today, and elected to ride in with the two pilots and bombardier. The belly-landing was so smooth the only damage was a slightly bent prop.

The real news of the day, however, was the reception committee awaiting us when we landed: a covey of uniformed Red Cross gals, armed with cold juice and cookies. And smiles.

Los Negros, Admiralty Islands, July 10—Again we fly to Yap, and again it is a tilt against fearsome, undaunted aerial lancers. I watch one who appears to richochet off the sun in his plunge towards us. When his path of flight is interrupted by the flash and smoke of our guns, he lifts a wing and falls off to the side, as a bird faking an injury. When I next see him he is streaking upward in a tight spiral, attempting to regain his perch in the blinding light of the protecting sun.

Our bombs fall soundlessly towards a cluster of island specks so far below they are not even brushed by the shadows of our wings.

Murphy and I take turns watching the automatic pilot fly us home. When it is his turn, I close my eyes and imagine we are flying underwater, in the seven mile deep canyon of the Marianna Trench. Hans says it is out here somewhere. In my daydream, we fly through the green-blue water with landing lights on, scattering schools of exotic, brightly colored fish.

But for most of the six hours it takes to fly back, I stare at the horizon, listening to the synchronized roar of four engines in one ear, radio static in the other, dreaming, always, of when this will all end.

* * *

The Red Cross girls did not meet our planes at the hardstands this afternoon, but they were at the de-briefing tent. Juice and cookies, too.

Los Negros, Admiralty Islands, July 15—Weather frustrated today's rendezvous at the Sorol Islands, causing us to find Yap on our own. We were almost over the island itself when we emerged from the clouds, then to be met by a plague of Zekes. It was too late to find formation positions so we bunched together as best we could then bombed at will. The Zekes, uncharacteristically, waited until our bomb-bays were empty before launching their usual frenzied attack. We fought them off for the next 30 minutes. I saw two knocked out of the sky: they fell like burned out rockets.

One of our planes was badly shot up and had to ditch. It had two engines out, a runaway prop on the third, and almost no fuel left. I heard this much on the radio, from the pilot's call for help. Later, only five members of the crew could be seen in rafts. A "Dumbo" was sent to pick them up and look for the others. Meantime, I heard a radio report that two 5th Group planes had unexplainably collided and fallen into the sea. No parachutes were seen and all 20 men were presumed lost.

No Red Cross girls at the hardstands *or* the de-briefing tent when we returned to Mokerang Field. Just the juice and cookies. Who needs a waitress? Who needs the Red Cross?

Los Negros, Admiralty Islands, July 16—This base is beginning to resemble a stateside training facility. There is piped-in music at the Mess Hall for dinner, sometimes even a free bottle of beer for the asking to drink with the ever more frequent meal of fresh foods.

The Officers Club has a newly poured cement floor, indirect lighting at the bar, an unlimited supply of free nuts to snack on; and, last night for the first time ever, lady customers! I walked in after the movie to be blinded by the sight of two Army nurses sitting at one of the tables. Their escorts, unfortunately, were *ground* officers, but we flyers are up to the challenge. Meantime, many questions are posed: Will nurses be permanent fixtures here on the base? Or just occasional visitors? Will a dress code be enforced at the Club? Explicit language forbidden at the crap table? Will the one-hole privy behind the Club be a ladies-only establishment on designated nights?

Meantime, of course, life goes on: the missions get longer, the enemy fighter pilots more aggressive, the anti-aircraft fire more accurate, the tropical storms more unpredictable and destructive, the sun hotter, the daily rains heavier, the mosquitoes more tenacious. And why, these last few weeks, do memories of home seem less vivid, familiar voices more muffled, remembered faces always slowly turn away?

Los Negros, Admiralty Islands, July 21—I am beginning to realize that the letters I write are elements of a novel I am composing in my mind. In some instances, the letter is addressed to a character in the novel who will give me the response I need for the story. But many of the letters are important only because they tell something about me. They could be addressed to anyone. They clarify and refine my role. Sometimes, such a letter will describe a plane falling from the sky; or tell of watching a circular rainbow form around a cloud. These are exercises, as one would practice sketching or experiment with a new color palette.

The notebook of story ideas I keep is another "voice" of the novel, one oblivious of all censors—including myself—and ignorant of the sensibilities of the persons discussed. Even the "truth" known to family and friends is flaunted. But my true fears, my naked feelings are most likely found between lines in the letters, not the notebook.

An actual writing project, while I'm here, seems impossible. I keep a "Mary-Jane" section in the notebook for the story of Gwicky and his crew. All I have written so far are the "facts." Gwicky as a real person still eludes me. His three tentmates and flight deck companions are mere ciphers. I must replace them with people I know. Individuals who come to mind are all from University days: Janzer, Roessler, John Bick, even Dupee. Only Janzer was a close friend. Ben himself is perfectly cast as the S-2 officer who spends a night in the tent of the missing men, reading their secret letters and painful diaries.

Also unwritten and, at this time, unwriteable, is the piece Martha proposed for a Sam Barber project, an account of my "deaths and entrances" as a flyer, the soliloquy of a man speaking to a woman across a great distance of his thoughts of love and fear and sorrow and happiness. I have not written a line of it—except, possibly, in letters.

* * *

Now it is late. I must find sleep soon if I am to rise before sunup. No music to make it easier; only the surf sounds on the beach below, the rattling of fronds in the palms overhead. I turn on my bed to follow the path of the moon eastward.

Los Negros, Admiralty Islands, July 22—Leaving the de-briefing tent this afternoon I noticed a crowd milling about at the Group bulletin board. These two headlines were the reason:

TOJO RESIGNS JAPANESE PREMIER POST

DEMOCRATS RE-NOMINATE FDR FOR
PRESIDENT
Harry Truman To Be His Running Mate

Ben says the Tojo resignation, if true, is a portentous development. "But who is Harry Truman?" he wanted to know. I could not enlighten him.

* * *

We hit targets on the island Tamil-Gagil today. Only a narrow canal separates it from Yap. Purpose of the raid was to keep Yap planes from flying north where US forces were invading Guam.

The GI, whose letters to pianist Robert Casadesus I was secretly monitoring, got evacuated to a rear-area hospital for treatment of a tropical disease while I was in Sydney. So Ben informed me when I inquired about the correspondence. Some bug he picked up at one of those native villages he visited, Ben guessed.

Los Negros, Admiralty Islands, August 2—Today I flew with Roy Grover and his crew in a plane called "Sugar Babe." No wonder we had problems!

The target was Woleai, one of those little atolls in the Yap group. It was my third trip there. Anti-aircraft fire was heavier than I remembered. I thought we had lucked our way through those innocent looking smoke puffs, but asked the crew to make a visual check of all surfaces, just in case. The report was negative.

So we thought. An hour later the flight engineer found gasoline dripping from somewhere along the bomb bay ceiling down to the catwalk. He said the fumes were intense. As we all knew, one flick of a Zippo lighter would blow us out of the sky. Grover had me alert the crew and warn each member by intercom not to light up. The gas fumes were beginning to spread throughout the ship.

Meantime, the engineer gingerly cranked open the bomb bay doors by hand—a long and tedious process, but necessary because the servomotor normally used might throw a spark. Once the doors were open, the fumes began venting to the outside.

The engineer then came up with an ingenious means of diverting the dripping gasoline to the outside of the plane. He fashioned a funnel from an inverted gun-oil can with its bottom cut out, and attached an oxygen hose to the can's spout. Several lengths of hose, taped together, were added until the tube reached an opening under the retracted ball turret, where the end of the hose could dangle outside the plane and drain off the leaking fuel.

All during the hours it took for the gasoline to stop dripping and the fumes to dissipate, I worried that someone might be tempted to light a cigarette, unobserved, in one of the gun turrets, behind a bulkhead—there are so many hidden corners and passages in a plane. Later, I was embarrassed by my concern. Long before I saw the towering mass of clouds that permanently hangs over Los Negros, the gas leak had stopped, opened hatches and windows had let in fresh air to flush away the gas fumes, and I had not once smelled the sweet aroma of cigarette smoke. We had safely returned to Mokerang Field in a plane called "Sugar Babe."

Los Negros, Admiralty Islands, August 8—The monthly "Going Home" list was posted today. I am No. 3 for pilots. When I am No. 1, and a replacement for me is here, I get to go home. As of July 31, when this list was drawn up, I had 36 strikes, 345 hours of combat flying, and nine months overseas. I've added two more strikes since the 31st—both to Yap, and 25 more combat flying hours.

* * *

The "Mosquito Radio Network," broadcasting from Guadalcanal to all US bases in the South Pacific, reports today that Antoine de St. Exupery is missing on a reconnaisance flight over southern France. He is in his 40s but somehow talked the Free French authorities into putting him on active duty flying status. His novel, *Night Flight*, is one of my favorite books. He's the only writer I know who can translate the sensation of flying into words that are meaningful to other flyers.

Los Negros, Admiralty Islands, August 10—Martha writes from Bennington College where she and her Company are in residence for the summer. *Penitente, Deaths and Entrances* and *Circus* were to be performed this weekend. Martha is also working on a new piece with music by Aaron Copland. She says the score has a "small town scale, a feeling of Sabbath."

The rehearsals, as usual, are in the little gymnasium-like room called the "Bear Pit." Martha says it was here she first saw me. I was in a technique class being taught by Ethel Butler. I had arrived at Bennington the day before, from Madison, Wisconsin, having just graduated from the University.

It is mid-day, July 1, 1940, as I step down from the bus while it hesitates at the curb of a downtown street, its engine still running. The driver assures me this is, indeed, Bennington, Vermont, my destination. He retrieves my heavy, leather suitcase from the luggage compartment. (It contains all my worldly possessions, except the Corona portable typewriter, which I hand-carry.)

The bus departs with an explosive snarl. I am left alone on the sidewalk of this unfamiliar town. A factory whistle stirs the summer heat with its noontime blast.

I am armed only with a letter assuring me I am expected and will be met here at the bus stop and driven to the college. And congratulating me for having won a dance scholarship. Still, I wonder and worry, waiting, clutching the stub of a one-way bus ticket that has stranded me here.

Los Negros, Admiralty Islands, August 13—It is Sunday. Today's headline on the Group bulletin board reads: ALLIES CAPTURE FLORENCE, ITALY.

I have not flown a strike in five days but did, finally, get off the ground today to co-pilot a ferry flight to the island Wakde, four hours due west of here. Wakde is rumored to be the site of our next base. The plane was loaded with Headquarters supplies for Operations and S-2 instead of bombs. Imagine using a four-engine bomber to transport office supplies!

If Wakde is truly to be our new home, I did not like what I saw today. It is a very small island, flat, nearly treeless. The runway cuts down the middle, beginning and ending at water. One can see the coast of Dutch New Guinea a few miles off to the west.

The place is still in bad shape from last May's invasion by US troops. Rubble everywhere, bull-dozed into large piles to make room for roads and camp sites. The few trees left standing are stripped of their fronds. No grasses or undergrowth of any kind. Only brown sand, everywhere. I am not looking forward to living in a place like this.

We returned to Los Negros in time for an extravagant cookout on the beach below our tent. Three naval officers, friends of one of our pilots, all from Omaha, came to visit carrying 30 T-bone steaks. Dick Gilbert played chef. The steaks were first massaged with a mixture of butter, beer and salt and pepper, then broiled over wood coals. Twelve of us ate all 30 steaks and toasted homemade bread to the accompaniment of warm Wisconsin beer.

* * *

A copy of Mallarmé's poem *Herodiade* came in today's mail, sent by Martha as promised. But not the diagram she said Joseph Campbell, Jean

Erdman's husband, had devised to help her better understand the poem. She described it, on first reading, as "strange, beautiful and repellent." Hindemith was commissioned by the Coolidge Foundation to write a musical score for her, and insisted that her ballet be based on this poem. Martha had wanted to do a piece with Cordelia, of *King Lear*, as her inspiration. (I read in the current *Time* magazine that Joe Campbell has co-authored a newly published book, *Skeleton Key to Finnegan's Wake*.)

Los Negros, Admiralty Islands, August 16—Censorship rules have been somewhat relaxed. We are now permitted to say in letters where we bombed yesterday, where we lived last week, and may name the islands we have seen in the past. No mention of today's activities or destinations, or anything planned for tomorrow.

  Prisoner-of-war conduct has also been modified. If we are lucky enough to survive a parachute jump into a jungle, or a ditching at sea, and unlucky enough to be captured by the Japanese, we will live longer if, (a) we tell our interrogators everything they want to know that we are entitled to know in our particular jobs, because they probably already know all about that sort of thing; and, (b) can string together a sweaty and lengthy account of our real or imagined sexual prowess, a subject that presumably fascinates the Japanese. A uniformed emissary of rank came all the way from Washington to tell us this. He said the "name-rank-serial number-only" routine no longer works out here. It quickly ends the interrogation, sometimes with fatal consequences. The current strategy is to say things that will intrigue our captors to the extent that we are sent farther and farther back from the fighting front, where food is in short supply for soldiers, much less prisoners of war. It is in the rear area that security will be somewhat more relaxed and we would have a better chance to escape. So the man says.

* * *

  Had another "cargo" flight to Wakde yesterday. Still don't like the place. Have two more trips coming up. Is it a shortage of C-47s that has turned a bomber squadron into a long-haul moving company? Or has Bomber Command run out of targets?

Los Negros, Admiralty Islands, August 20—Tomorrow morning, all flight crews take off for Wakde Island, the newest 13th Air Force South Pacific base. Hopefully, it will be my last "home" out here.

  I am more reluctant than ever to leave Los Negros having seen, yesterday, the Wakde campsite. It is on a barren, thumb-like peninsula that juts out the northwest corner of the island. The coast of Dutch New Guinea can be seen in the distance. But the view from our tent will not be New Guinea or even the water surrounding the tiny island, only hundreds of other tents—a "sea" of tents, on a barren plain of hot, brown sand.

No trees will shade our blistering canvas shelters by day, or hide birds and animals whose occasional cries at night remind us of where we are.

* * *

I take a long, last look at the beach below our Los Negros "Tree House" where for the past four months I have been able to look down on the rolling surf washing over the glistening, white sand, lighted sometimes only by the stars. The towering, unbending palms stand guard on the embankment, their fronds gently swaying and rustling in the rising, sea-sweet night breeze.

WAKDE

It took only two days for troops of the US 41st Division, under the command of Gen. Robert Eichelberger, to wrest tiny Wakde Island from its Japanese defenders but the fighting was fierce, continuous and often hand-to-hand. By the time the shooting stopped, May 19, 1944, only one Japanese prisoner had been taken alive. Gen. Eichelberger tells us that a Japanese Marine walked into a supply dump, hands raised, and asked, in perfect English, to surrender. He said he had been born and raised in Hawaii.

When our troops went ashore, May 17, 1944, they saw only a deserted airfield. No Japanese were in sight. However, the enemy was soon discovered, underground, hiding in some 100 bomb-proof bunkers and 12 large caves. Tanks were needed to dislodge the Japanese. The airstrip was bull-dozed back into shape even as the fighting continued, and was ready for use on D+4 days. The first US planes to take off flew an aerial reconnaissance mission to the southern Philippines.

Wakde is a mere 9,000 feet long, a mile wide. It lies within sight of the Dutch New Guinea coast, midway between Hollandia, MacArthur's Headquarters, and the island of Biak. MacArthur considered Wakde more suitable than Hollandia for development into a strategically important air base.

The price for taking Wakde was, thankfully, only 40 US infantrymen dead. More than 800 comrades of that one English-speaking Japanese Marine died defending the tiny, now desolate, tree-less, scarred patch of sand and battle debris.

Wakde, August 21—Our sea-breezed canvas aerie that hung high above a glistening beach on Los Negros has been replaced by an unshaded, fly-collecting tent pitched over a floor of sand. It is lighted at night only by spluttering candles. (An electricity-producing generator for the squadron is forever promised by sundown tomorrow.) The tents are in rigid rows across a bleak, tree-less peninsula jutting from the island's western shore. The runway, running north and south, splitting the island in half, is alive with the sight and sound of planes constantly landing and taking off.

Wakde resembles no island I've lived on or visited, only some I've bombed. It approximates the Hollywood version of a newly captured Jap base: the few palm trees still standing wear tattered crowns and shattered trunks; disused Jap foxholes and slit-trenches gape menacingly on all sides; piles of smashed guns, vehicles and other equipment—the detrius of war— have still to be bull-dozed into the sea. Wreckage of one Zeke plane is of special interest to those of us who have only seen it at 20-thousand feet, trying to shoot us down. It's unusual to arrive at a new base this soon, before it's been picked clean of "souvenirs."

But as always, when we first arrive, life proceeds on a somewhat prim-itive (for us) level: meals are eaten from mess kits; drinking water, tepid and tasting of iodine, comes from hanging canvas Lister bags; showers are available only to those who wait in line for the one designated hour a day the precious sun-warmed fresh water is dispensed from a P-38 belly gas tank on a raised platform. There's no PX, no Officers Club, no cigarettes. Most depressing of all, I'm 600 miles farther from home . . .

Wakde, August 25—Today's mission, the first from here, took us 750 miles northwest to the Palau islands in the Western Carolines. We were the first 13th Air Force planes to bomb targets there. This is where the Jap-anese have concentrated naval forces to guard approaches to the Philip-pines, 500 miles to the west.

We were told to look for shipping of any kind in Malakal Harbor at Koror but found only a cluster of barges lashed together. Our bombs missed, and Grover told the bombardier, Bloom, he needed more practice hitting barn doors

This is a newly-formed crew I have joined, and Grover and Les Bloom, the bombardier, are minor celebrities. Both survived a much publicized, disastrous mission to Rabaul last January 1st. Their plane, "Blessed Event," which Grover was co-piloting, was so badly shot up by Jap fighters that when it finally skidded to an emergency landing on Bougainville it was carrying two men dead and eight wounded, including the pilot, co-pilot Grover and bombardier Bloom.

We are the "oldest" crew in the squadron if one counts our cumulative time overseas. The "youngest" member is navigator Hans Meier, Pete's original replacement last June when he and Murphy went home. Meier is a stubborn, argumentative Dutchman for whom everything is either "right" or "wrong," "black" or "white." There are no "in betweens," no gradations, no such thing as a "compromise." He is a good enough navigator but everything is done "by the book," sometimes to the peril of the crew. He once took us home from Biak on a straight-line course which had us fly over a couple of innocent-looking small islands. We suddenly found ourselves the target of intense anti-aircraft fire, some of which found "Frenisi's" tail. We almost threw Meier out of the plane. Pete was still around and we had him give Meier a little lecture about not plotting short-cut courses over unknown islands.

Grover is a quiet, very controlled, deadly serious fellow. Judging from the two missions I have flown as his co-pilot, I know he will be a careful, supremely efficient airplane commander. I doubt if I will ever get to know him personally, and we will not spend much time together on the ground. But it will be a pleasure to fly with someone as calm and knowledgeable about airplanes as Grover. I will long remember with astonishment how he brought us back from Woleai with gas dripping into the bomb bay, just as if it was an everyday occurrence.

Bloom is from Brooklyn, a chunky, happy-go-lucky fellow, untroubled by the heat, the mosquitoes, the enemy. Only the quality—and quantity—of food served in the mess hall concerns him. And music of any and all kinds. Food and music are Bloom's passions.

I do not know any of the enlisted men personally, though I have a nodding acquaintance with several who substituted on "Frenisi" crews. All seem extremely professional, all are "old timers," resigned to their fate. There was no horsing around today, no idle chatter on the intercom, no sleeping in the turrets.

39 strikes and counting.

* * *

We learned at de-briefing this afternoon that Nazi forces holding Paris have surrendered unconditionally to allied commanders.

Wakde, August 26—A P-38 outfit was already here on Wakde when we arrived. Those hot-shot pilots still act as if we B-24 drivers are intruding on their turf. First couple of days they delighted in blowing down our tents with the wash of their twin props. They'd fly in low over the camp, pull straight up over the tents. Their wash would turn the tents inside out and scatter our personal stuff to kingdom come. Finally, our major talked to their major and the horseplay stopped.

But not their showing-off. Whenever they return from a successful mission, they put on the best airshow in town. Today, for example, one of the returning '38s buzzed the runway at prop level. We ran over to the field from our nearby tent to see what was coming next. The guy first pulled straight up and began arcing over into a big loop. At the top of the loop, directly over the field, he cut his two engines, feathered the props, dropping his landing gear as he plummeted down on the back side of the loop. He pulled out just in time to grease the plane in for a perfect dead-stick landing.

I remember a time when I had dreams of flying like that P-38 pilot . . .

It is March of 1942, and I am hanging face-down in the open cockpit of an upside down Stearman primary trainer, praying the safety belt will keep me from falling out and down into the South Carolina cotton field perilously far below. Without warning, instructor Johnston flips the plane rightside up. "Half roll to the right!" he yells into the speaking tube. The plane's little engine groans as it struggles to keep the ship flying level. "Snap-roll to the left!" I now hear. Over we go. We're flying rightside up and straight and level, for a change. Johnston aims us for a massive pile of clouds. "Chandelle!" he announces, jerking the stick all the way back. I take my hands off my duplicate set of controls; they're moving too fast! Now we're in a vertical climb, slowly spiraling, hanging from the propeller. Just as the plane is about to fall off on a wing, Johnston jams the stick forward and kicks right rudder. I'm thrown against the back of the seat by the sharp turn. "We've lost him!" Johnston gleefully shouts. He waggles the wings at our mythical enemy. Then, without warning, we're diving again. "Immelman!" he shouts. I'm thrust forward against the safety belt, then slammed back, as we begin another vertical climb. The engine screams in protest. At the top of this half-loop, Johnston snap-rolls us over to rightside up. "Got him in our sights!" my instructor-cum Eddie Rickenbacker chortles. We take off in hot pursuit. I place both hands back on the stick, the thumb of my right hand is on the make-believe trigger button. Now I, too, have the Baron in my sights!

Wakde, August 29—I escaped the still-sweltering tent after dinner to join Ben in his Jeep to trace the island's perimeter roads in search of cooling breezes to erase the memory of seeing one of our planes shot down over Pelieu this morning.

The southern end of the runway terminates at the edge of a cliff. We park on the beach below and watch a night-flying Snooper plane vault into the air between sea and sky to begin its dusk-to-dawn patrol.

We tarry to marvel as feathered clouds, drifting past the descending sun, become multi-colored flaming quills. Streaks of lightning knife unheard through massive cloud-mountains of billowing grays and blues.

We resume our perambulation, now at water's edge, on hard-packed moist beach sand, scattering ribbons of spun foam abandoned by the retreating surf. The twilight colors are suffused by the descending darkness. We pass near our tethered planes in their lonely revetments, now guarded only by a scattering of forlorn, tattered palm trees.

The stars alone light our way back across the island's moonscape. I must count the tents to find my own in the shadowy row. Just beyond, in a small cove, three abandoned LST's languish in the shallow water like giant beached whales.

Inside the tent, I find my cot in a corner of the flickering splash of candlelight and prepare to confront the night.

40 missions. Still counting.

Wakde, September 1—The "Going Home" list is posted today. I'm ranked 2nd among all pilots in the squadron for total points earned by the end of August.

I'm now credited with 40 strikes, 500 combat hours, and ten months overseas.

I'm only .6 of a point behind the No. 1 man. But the No. 3 pilot on the list is only .1 of a point behind me!

* * *

Continue reading Proust to keep my mind off "points." Finished *The Captive* last night; am now beginning *The Fugitive*. But with Pete back in the States, there's no one to talk to about Proust . . .

Wakde, September 2—The Palau Islands, 750 miles to the northwest, are now our primary targets. They guard the approaches to the Philippines. Peleliu in particular. Koror island, also heavily fortified, is headquarters for all military forces in the area.

The Briefing Officer, old friend Ben, told us that before the war Koror was a major tourist site for the Japanese, their Pacific "Riviera," where they would luxuriate on dazzling white sand beaches and cruise among the so-called Rock Islands, hundreds of tiny, jungle-covered, green, knob-like formations appearing to float on the water. "Emerald mushrooms popping up above a calm blue sea," was the translated description Ben read to us from an old Japanese tourist guide.

Today's mission was to Koror to bomb its military installations—storage facilities and anti-aircraft batteries in and near Koror town.

Just as I turned the plane for the bomb run, I saw the sun begin its rise from the sea—and would have halted us in mid-flight if that had been possible, to watch the sun's majestic ascension. Iridescent dew bathed the pale blue island we were crossing, Babelthuap, and night mists were lifting, revealing trees and streams and soft, meadow-like fields. Then, as I stared in wonderment, a giant rainbow began to form. I guided the plane towards its arch and held my breath.

Bombs were soon falling from our planes, mortally wounding the green, moist, sleepy little island of Koror below, staining it with blood-red tears of fire. I could see, just beyond the town, the strings of "emerald mushrooms" floating on the calm blue sea.

* * *

I have written my "good-night" letter—as one would tell his beads. A piece of the moon is overhead, a slice of just-peeled orange, Proust would say. Fluffy, white clouds hold it against the blue-black sky. All this quieting beauty to mask the reason I am here.

Wakde, September 3—I awake mid-morning to the chime-like tinkle of a hanging Japanese brake drum being struck. It quickly stills the laughter-tinged chatter in the chapel tent across the way. The chanted monotone of a prayer holds the voices quiet. I can see rows of bowed heads from where I lie on my cot. The muted tone of a pitchpipe offers the first note of a hymn. I hear the young men singing, quietly, hesitantly—as if expecting, hoping, to hear a soprano or a contralto joining them . . .

I miss the sopranos and contraltos, too.

* * *

This is the beginning of a glistening, airless day. I walk the unshaded, sand-clogged path to Ben's tent to share my loneliness. He's not there.

I return to my tent and the solace of my mosquito net-shrouded cot. The remains of the chapel service drones on as I cherish the memory of sopranos and contraltos I have known. And loved.

Wakde, September 4—Had an unscheduled return to the Palaus today on a mission of mercy. We were sent to look for the crew of a downed B-24, thought to have ditched, or crashed, in waters off Babelthuap island. We could spare only enough fuel for an hour's search, ever mindful of how much we would need for the long flight back to Wakde.

We did not find any signs of the ten men or their plane: no rafts, no floating oxygen bottles, no torn strips of aluminum, no oil slicks; only the blue-gray Philippine Sea from horizon to horizon and the pencil-line coast of Babelthuap in the distance.

Could the men have been picked up by the Japanese? Would we ever know?

We crept back to Wakde in the silence of our failure.

* * *

I finished the final volume of Proust a few moments ago. I shall have to invent another life to dwell in while tethered to this island. Flying is no longer enough.

Wakde, September 5—Two so-called "big" shows recently found this tiny island. I avoided both. I find such entertainments ill-disguised attempts to make our life out here more tolerable. I resent that. Life out here is meant to be intolerable. Nothing—no one—can make it otherwise.

Those who do not share my view—hundreds of them—waited two hours under the near-vertical burning sun to secure seats near the stage and performers Bob Hope, Frances Langford, and Jerry Colona. They heard Hope say: "I love this beautiful island, with its magnificent palm trees . . . two of them with tops."

The unlikely star attraction of the other "entertainment" some days later, which I also avoided, was actress Judith Anderson, reading Shakespeare. A violinist and singer, whose names I never saw posted, shared the sunburned stage. There was no crush for front-row seats to this inappropriate event.

* * *

I'm informed that the sun is approaching its zenith. It never goes below 27 degrees from the vertical over Wakde. Of course, we are less than two degrees below the equator, and we always get burned, never tanned, if we linger at the beach.

Wakde, September 6—All first pilots got orders the other day to sign up for a refresher course in night landings. Why? We take off in the dark on almost every strike but always land during daylight hours. What does Bomber Command have planned for us?

The first session was held tonight. I flew co-pilot in one of the six planes taking part. Three first pilots were assigned to each plane and took turns shooting the landings. Had to do three before calling it a night.

One of the pilots in my plane finally finished his three and a second pilot took the seat to begin his round. We lined up for takeoff a little off to the side of the runway and waited for the plane coming in to land. I watched the final approach: he was in a steep glide with full flaps, wheels down, landing lights sweeping the runway ahead. But the plane did not land, just leveled off and continued flying straight and level the length of the runway, finally disappearing from sight.

We stayed where we were and waited for instructions from the Tower. A few minutes later the Tower said we were all to come in. Said that the plane we were watching had flown straight into the sea. There would be no more takeoffs and landings this night. Or ever, I thought to myself, for the three pilots, the co-pilot and the flight engineer aboard that plane.

Wakde, September 7—Today is Dad's 53rd birthday. We were last together a year ago, in late July, at Turner Field, Albany, Georgia. He'd come all the way from Wisconsin by train to pin on my Pilot Wings and congratulate me for graduating from flight school and receiving my commission in the Air Force. The next day I left for Maxwell Field in Alabama to begin B-24 training; Dad headed back to Wisconsin Rapids.

Dad's beginning his 18th year as principal of a small teachers' training school. It offers a two year degree program for high school graduates who want to become teachers in rural one-room schools. As I recall, they could look forward to being paid about $75 a month, and boarding free at someone's farmhouse in the district.

I think of Mother, too. She would have been 54 years old the 27th of next month.

It's early summer, 1927. Mother and brother Rob and I have just arrived by train at the Wisconsin Rapids station. We have come from the even smaller town of Alma, on the banks of the Mississippi River, to join Dad, who has a new job at a larger school here. A small group of children are on the station platform with baskets of wild flowers for sale. One penny per bunch. We do not see Dad. Then we hear him calling to us: "Louise!" "Boys!" We rush to find him. He hands Mother a bouquet of the wild flowers. I put my arm around one of his legs; he tousles my hair. We follow him to the Model-T I remember from Alma. He drives us to our new home on Elm Street.

* * *

It's now two years later; the morning of March 22. I'm a 7th grader, and at my desk in the one-room simulated rural school where my father's students practice teaching. Rob's a 4th grader and sits in a row of smaller desks on the opposite side of the room. The clock on the wall behind Miss Ganz, our teacher, reads ten minutes past 10:00. A man enters the room, goes directly to Miss Ganz and whispers something to her. She puts her hand to her mouth, then quietly calls my name, then Rob's, and beckons us to come to her desk. She tells us that our mother has taken a turn for the worse, and we are to go home, that my father is already there. The man, whom I recognize as one of the student teachers, will drive us. We follow him out of the classroom.

Dad meets us at the front door. He takes us by the hand, and we walk up the stairway in silence. He guides us to the front bedroom, where Mother has been in bed so many weeks. Dad opens the door but holds us back from entering. I see a man standing by the bed—the doctor? There's a form on the bed, wrapped in a sheet. All the bedclothes have been removed. The man pulls out a corner of the sheet wrapped around the form on the bed and looks underneath. Dad quickly pulls us back and closes the door. We go back down stairs.

I learn in the following days that Mother's death was caused by lung cancer. She was thought to be suffering from tuberculosis. She was 39 years old.

Wakde, September 15—We dropped one-ton "blockbuster" bombs on Halmahara's Lolobata Airfield today. At the same time, US troops invaded Morotai, a small island just 11 miles off the northeast coast of Halmahara. Our land forces are now within 300 miles of the Philippines.

Meantime, US Marines landed on the island of Peleliu, in the Palaus, which we bombed last month.

* * *

The base radio station last night picked up a report on short wave that Germany has surrendered. The news spread throughout the camp in minutes. Spontaneous celebrations erupted. O'Toole's co-pilot, Shedd, was so happy—and drunk—he shot himself in the hand. Today we learned that Germany has *not* surrendered. And Shedd is grounded with a badly mangled hand.

Wakde, September 18—Today's mission was to Ceram, a place where I once looked forward to seeing gold-roofed temples, glinting in the sun, not rapacious Zekes we were warned to expect in swarms. I saw neither.

The outbound flight was at a lower than usual altitude, over trackless jungles in western New Guinea and vast, grassy plains and rolling hills of the Vogelkop. We were instructed to look for signs of Japanese occupation but saw none, only occasional glimpses of tiny thatched huts, on stilts, clustered along the shore of a hidden cove; and sometimes delicate strands of pale gray smoke twisting skyward from the depths of a forest; and once a long chain of toy-like dugout canoes tracing loops and arcs on a mirrored lake.

We found our bombing target on Haroeko, a small island off the eastern-most tip of Ceram. Its airfield, positioned to protect Jap-held oil fields farther north at Bula Bay, appeared deserted, possibly abandoned. Even the anti-aircraft guns were silent. We dropped our bombs, regardless, and headed back across the Ceram Sea for home. Well, Wakde.

As I left the de-briefing tent, after the mission, Dick Gilbert came up to me, gripped my hand, and told me I had flown my last combat mission. It was No. 46.

No more counting.

NOEMFOOR

General MacArthur's feints and assaults on Japanese-held bases during the summer of 1944 followed a northwest path leading inexorably to the Philippines. One of these was the little-known island Noemfoor which fell to US paratroopers on July 2 and soon became the most advanced allied bomber base in the Pacific. It is just 850 miles from Mindanao.

Elliptically shaped, roughly 11 miles in diameter, Noemfoor is one of the Schouten Islands and lies 90 miles west of Biak. It is encircled by a jagged fringe of coral reefs that prevent most approaches from the sea.

Japanese troops arrived in November of 1943, but unable to recruit local natives to build their airfields, they imported 3,000 men, women and children from Java. When US paratroopers landed eight months later only 403 Javanese were still alive; but three airfields completed.

The first battalion of US paratroopers dropped on July 2, 1944, suffered 72 jump casualties; the second battalion dropped added 56 more. The remaining troopers were airlifted in. Mopping-up operations were concluded by the end of August. There were reports that the defeated, starving enemy had resorted to "promiscuous" cannibalism.

Noemfoor, September 28—This could be my last Pacific island home, but not one I will want to remember for any other reason. I've been here only three days but already I find Noemfoor a depressing, makeshift, uncomfortable place, and have every indication it will remain this way—a temporary base, soon to be abandoned for one even closer to the Philippines.

The tent I share with three strangers slouches in a clearcut section of the jungle, now unnecessarily exposed to the blistering sun, and pitched over soft, spongy ground made almost soupy by the daily rains which flood across the dirt floor underneath our cots. When it is not raining, the parrot screams and locust drones barely stir the fetid air. Even treeless, scorching, fly-ridden, sand-blown Wakde now seems preferable. Heaven, in my dreams, is Los Negros and that aerial tent perched above surf and beach.

My three tentmates are newly arrived from the States, replacements not yet assigned to crews—a navigator, two bombardiers, anxious to fly their first combat mission. I have experienced their frustration. They do not know mine, being hobbled to the ground, my combat wings clipped, expecting to be joyous, saddened instead.

Noemfoor, September 29—I began the day astride a de-fanged B-24 co-piloting a five hour roundtrip cargo-run back to Wakde. What a delightfully disconcerting experience to be flying without having to constantly peer for Zekes in the clouds, and to be free of the steel flak helmet, the bullet-proof vest. Flying can still be enjoyable without all that gladiator gear.

We even passed near a long narrow island named "Japen" without trepidation.

We then aimed for Sarmi, on the Dutch New Guinea coast. When it was beneath us, there was Wakde, floating two miles off shore.

* * *

Back at Noemfoor, late this afternoon, I "audited" the briefing for tomorrow's "biggest, longest, most important" strike the 13th Air Force has ever flown. Only generals and colonels sat on the improvised stage. The target is Borneo's oil and gas refineries at Balikpapan, the "Ploesti" of the Far East. Seventy-two 13th Air Force B-24s will fly the 16 1/2 hour mission. There will be no fighter cover.

I learned in the course of the briefing that that disastrous night landing and takeoff "refresher" course on Wakde was intended to prepare pilots for these Balikpapan strikes, which will begin and end in the dark.

* * *

Pete writes that he got married on the 20th. Still plans to meet me in New York.

Noemfoor, September 30—I was at Konasoran Field by 3:30 this morning to watch the takeoff for Balikapapan. The usual sounds of dawn here—screeching gulls, breakers crashing on nearby reefs—could not be heard above the roar and whine and splutter of hundreds of airplane engines being started and revved up and idled. The scene, viewed from my perch on the roof of a truck cab, was of shadowy behemoths, wingtip lights slowly blinking, lurching towards the beginning of the runway.

At the other end of the mile-long airstrip, two huge searchlights were positioned on opposite sides of the runway, their light beams aimed directly at one another, forming a luminous bar some 25 feet off the ground. Pilots were warned they must vault their planes over this light bar on takeoff to be sufficiently airborne in time to avoid plunging into the sea a few hundred feet farther on. Bulldozers with engines snarling waited at the edge of the tarmac, should a plane falter and fall and have to be pushed off the runway.

When they finally came, at $1^{1}/_{2}$-minute intervals, all 72 planes made it over the light bar into the air. One scraped its bomb-bay doors on the runway's packed coral surface but managed to maintain sufficient forward thrust to continue on up into the still-darkened sky.

* * *

Sixteen hours later, I was back at Kornasoren, now quiet and deserted except for small clusters of crew chiefs and mechanics at the empty hardstands. Some stared at the empty, darkening sky, as I did, for the sight of a returning plane; others, sitting on empty bomb crates, heads down, appeared to be listening for the sound of a B-24.

I parked my borrowed jeep at the Operations shack where a loudspeaker was spluttering with static and, occasionally, with voices so garbled and distorted as to be unintelligible. Then there were long silent pauses during which the Operations radioman would repeat his call: "Bravo! Bravo! Do you hear me? Come in, Bravo!" There was never an answer, only the static and scrambled voices.

I went outside to again search the sky, now stained with the vermillion wash of the dying sunset. I felt suffocated by a feeling of guilt, being here, safe on the ground, not out there, somewhere, with "them," sharing their fears and pain.

An hour or so later, sometime after 9:00, an officer at one of the desks put down his phone and looked at those of us waiting. He said no planes would be returning to Noemfoor tonight. Those which had not already landed at Morotai or Sansapor would be out of gas. And down, ditched or crashed. The Dumbos would be out looking for them at dawn. The officer said he had no numbers but he did know that many of the planes now at Morotai and Sansapor had come in with empty gas tanks, feathered props, shattered tails, and, I knew, bleeding dead and wounded crewmen. He said a list of those planes and men unaccounted for and presumed "missing" would be posted in the morning.

* * *

My tent was one of the few in camp still lighted. My tentmates, whom I had met only a few days ago, put down their cards and stared at me, unbelieving, as I talked, and asked, again and again, "Not even *one* plane got back?" Not one, I said, knowing these three newly arrived flyers were scheduled to fly the next Balikpapan strike. Someone switched off the light and I slipped under the mosquito net to lie stretched out on top of the blankets. For the remainder of the night I endured dreams of lost, pilotless airplanes circling in a black, empty sky; endlessly, silently circling.

* * *

The unofficial report on yesterday's strike: Only 46 of the 72 planes got to Balikpapan. Four of those were shot down over the target. The remaining 42, most of them badly shot-up, limped back to either Morotai or Sansapor with their wounded, dying or dead crew members. The 26 planes that never made it to Balikpapan all had mechanical problems and landed at emergency fields en route to the target.

Noemfoor, October 5—The second Balikpapan strike, day before yesterday, was more disastrous than the first. Our Group lost seven of the 20 planes we sent along. All the other planes were damaged in some way. 63 men are still listed as missing. Ten others were pulled from the water by PBY "Dumbo" planes. One of the 28 injured men died of his wounds.

O'Toole led the mission. He volunteered—as did his crew—to fly even though they all were officially grounded and awaiting orders to go home. Only Shedd, their regular co-pilot, was not along. The hand he shot celebrating the false rumor of Germany's surrender was still not healed.

My newly-met tentmates were flying in planes of the second flight. It was their first combat mission. They told of seeing O'Toole's plane begin the bomb run, then, seconds later, burst into flames. It was hit by the first round of anti-aircraft fire. They said O'Toole kept his plane right on course for the bomb drop until it fell from the sky.

The planes my tentmates were in also got hit but no one was injured, and they managed to limp back as far as Middleburg for emergency repairs before returning, many hours later, to Noemfoor.

* * *

No detailed assessment yet of damage inflicted on the Balikpapan refineries. The unofficial word is: "Minimal."

Noemfoor, October 8—I fly very occasionally these days and then only to ferry war-weary B-24s to a deserted airstrip 850 miles southeast of here, at Nadzab. Planes only land there, never take off. We park the relics wingtip over wingtip, in endless rows, where they suffer the indignity of being stripped of reuseable parts. The flightless carcasses remaining will soon be ravaged by the encroaching jungle still wearing gaudy, painted noses emblazoned with racy portraits and saucy names, still proudly displaying neat rows of tiny painted bombs, one for each mission flown, *momento mori* for the crews who flew them.

I had no need today to look for "Frenisi," as I do each time I visit this depressing place. I had seen her earlier on Wakde during our refueling stop. She was grounded for want of a missing engine. I saluted her for having evaded that final flight to Nadzab one more time.

The plane we delivered to Nadzab today was being shorn of her equipment even before we disembarked. I watched a technician pry off the little metal cap from the hub of a control column wheel, thinking he wanted the wheel. What he did want—and found—was the name and phone number a Detroit assembly line girl had written inside the cap.

We delivered a new B-24-J to Wakde on the trip back, but missed the shuttle to Noemfoor and had to spend the night in one of those floorless, unscreened, candle-lit tents, fighting off sand flies. I hoped to share the misery with Ben, who had not moved with the rest of us to Noemfoor. However, as I soon learned, he had finally received his orders to go home and had left the island just two days before.

* * *

The memory of spending one last miserable night on Wakde, and the dread of an indefinite stay on the equally foreboding Noemfoor, is immediately dispelled on my return to Kornasoren Field the next morning. My name is on the list of those who will go home sometime *this* month.

Noemfoor, October 11—Les Bloom, bombardier on my last crew, also waiting to go home, today returned from a round-trip "whiskey-run" flight to Sydney. Somehow talked his way aboard. Brought back a stack of records including Shostakovich's *1st Symphony*. We borrowed a wind-up phonograph from Special Services and proceeded to introduce Shostakovich to the troops. More popular with the troops was an album of tantalizing songs sung by a Peggy Lee, an American singer unknown to most of us.

There is not much to occupy those of us grounded and awaiting orders to go home. No Officers Club, no Library, no volley ball courts. Worst of all, I have not received any mail since arriving here. I write answers to letters I only imagine I've received, then tear those up. I read and re-read the letters I have kept, especially those from Martha. I've tried and tried to begin writing the Gwicky story but never finish even a page. I *think* a lot about doing the piece Martha suggested, but now that I'm not flying I seem to have lost my voice—even the desire to write it.

Noemfoor, October 18—Flew back to Wakde last Friday, again with a war-weary B-24 for delivery to Nadzab. Also carried a load of spare engine parts Wakde had requisitioned. While waiting for the stuff to be unloaded, Operations suggested we two pilots arrange to stay on Wakde an extra day and get checked out in a C-47. We liked the idea and radioed Noemfoor for permission which was quickly granted.

As a consequence, Saturday was spent riding around with an Operations guy in an old, beat-up C-47, bouncing through uncounted landings and takeoffs. After passing a simple, no-fail, multiple-choice test, we were declared C-47 pilots. Operations said our names would be forwarded to Air Transport Command should it need more transport pilots during the Philippines invasion. I said I planned to watch the invasion from the Top of the Mark in San Francisco.

Sunday was spent delivering the old B-24 and gawking at a couple of pretty (I thought) WACs at the Nadzab PX, the first of their species seen in these parts. Thought about them Monday as we flew a silver B-24-J to Los Negros.

Alas, there was no time to visit old haunts on this most memorable of our island homes. I had especially wanted to take a last look at the "Tree

House," in memory still perched so beautifully, so precariously, out over the beach and surf. I did the next best thing—buzzed the place, at arm's length, on the ocean side, just after taking off for Noemfoor. After slowly dipping the wings, first the left, then the right, I climbed back up into the sky and headed westward into the sunset, aimed for Noemfoor.

* * *

When I returned to the tent tonight, the orders sending me home were on my cot. I fly to Nadzab in the morning. This trip will be one-way.

NADZAB

In the early morning hours of September 5, 1943, a fleet of some 90 C-47 transport planes, flying 12 abreast, shattered the stillness of beautiful Markham Valley in southern New Guinea. The planes followed an easterly course that bisected the graceful turns of the Markham River to a place called Nadzab, site of an abandoned airstrip constructed by the Australians before the war. Twenty miles farther to the east, smoke could be seen this day as it rose from the embattled Japanese-held seacoast town of Lae.

Leading this aerial armada was a B-17 carrying General Douglas Mac-Arthur and his Air Force Commander, General George Kenney. It was to be the first airborne assault in the Pacific by US paratroopers.

The US 503rd Parachute Regiment encountered no opposition to its jump from the low-flying planes. The airfield was quickly put back into commission for the next day's arrival of Australia's airborne 7th Division, which then joined the US paratroopers in assisting other allied forces in the battle at Lae. It took ten days of brutal fighting to recapture from the Japanese this one-time frontier town of gold miners.

Nadzab soon became a major air base for General Kenney's Fifth Air Force, but by mid-1944 it was relegated to serving as a terminal for all air routes leading to and from the United States and the air bases now on the approaches to the Philippines.

Nadzab, October 23—The invasion of Leyte, three days ago, is preventing my departure for San Francisco. Learned as soon as I arrived earlier today that all transport planes, large and small, are on standby for possible use in the Philippines operation. No one knows when a C-54 can be made available to the hundreds of us waiting to go home.

Meantime, must contend with conditions typical of every transient camp I have ever seen: floorless tents erected side by side on an open, dusty field miles from the airfield and other so-called "permanent" installations. It is as if we have been consigned to a large prisoner-of-war camp.

Worst of all, there are even rumors we will all be put aboard a troop ship as soon as one docks at Lae, twenty miles from here on the Huan Gulf.

Am told there is a movie only three times a week, no library or even a place to buy newspapers or magazines. In any event, the tents are not lighted.

Nadzab, October 25—A co-pilot I knew slightly while on Wakde and Noemfoor showed up at the mess hall today. Just in from Noemfoor. Said Balikpapan refinery strikes are on hold for the moment, all missions now concentrating on shipping in the Makassar Straits. Said hunting has been good; only one plane had been lost up to the time he left. That one simply vanished, he said. No one saw it go down. Searched and searched but found nothing. Said the crew was made up of volunteers, some already grounded and awaiting orders to go home. Only name he could remember, because he had flown with the guy a couple of times, was Bloom, the bombardier.

Of course. It had to be Bloom, the guy who introduced Shostakovitch *and* Peggy Lee to the troops on Noemfoor. He said he knew he had used up all his luck on that disastrous New Year's Day mission over Rabaul, when every member of the crew was either wounded or killed. His wounds in an arm, shoulder and leg had entitled him to a ground job. He refused to take one, explaining to me that regardless of where he was or what he was doing, he knew he would be found when the time came.

As apparently he was, off the coast of Borneo, on an October day in 1944 . . .

Nadzab, October 30—Day Seven. Still no planes leaving for the States except those carrying the wounded and dead from Leyte. The only rumor we hear is that we'll end up on a troopship.

The food is so bad everyone suffers from either diarrhea or constipation.

I'm still wearing the clothes I arrived in a week ago. No laundry; no place to wash clothes; no place to buy clothes.

Nadzab, November 1—The day was spent in Lae, 20 or so miles down the Markham Valley, on the shores of Huan Bay. Where that rumored troopship would dock, and take us home by way of Timbuktu. No troopship in dock today.

Several of us hitched a ride there in pursuit of a hamburger stand said to be in operation. It was, and we gorged ourselves on the hamburgers of whatever meat.

Not much to the town. First the Japs captured it, then the Aussies and us took it back, now the GIs have it. The place shows signs of mistreatment. Even the natives look out of place.

Pete had once told me that Lae was where Amelia Earhart took off on her last flight, the one to Howland Island that she never found. The 3,000-foot airstrip she used is right in the center of town, ending at the edge of a cliff overlooking the Bay. According to Pete, it was originally built in the '20s for small planes that ferried men and equipment to gold mines in the mountains.

Before leaving Lae, I stood at the far end of that little airstrip and tried to imagine Earhart's tiny silver plane out there over the Bay, turning on a course for Howland Island that July morning, seven years ago.

Nadzab, November 3—Today, met a 23-year-old major, a P-38 fighter pilot, who happens to come from Wisconsin. We have never visited one another's home town, do not know any of the same people, but coming from the same state is enough to make us buddies out here.

Terry is even more determined than most of us to leave this place in an airplane, not a troopship. Says he's checking out a rumor of another way to get home by plane.

His outfit up north is the one Charles Lindberg attached himself to for a couple of months to teach the pilots how to increase the range of their P-38s. Had to do with radically modifying air-fuel ratios. Terry says Lindberg managed to get in a couple of combat missions, too.

Nadzab, November 6—Terry's rumor turned out to be fact. There *is* a possible alternative to the C-54s and a troopship. He somehow learned that there are 75 B-25Hs at Townsville, Australia, waiting to be flown back to the States. Why not by us, says Terry?

This model of the B-25 has a 75mm cannon in the nose but no provision for a co-pilot. A couple of crews in the Fifth Air Force tried it out on missions but said "No thank you!": no provision for extra gas tanks, needed for the distances being flown; limited uses for the cannon instead of bombs. The crews felt a cannon was not a fair substitute for a co-pilot. The plane was rejected.

Terry thinks we should offer to fly them back to Wright Field for refunds.

Stay tuned.

Nadzab, November 9—Terry and I hitched a ride back to Hollandia this morning, he hoping to find someone at Air Transport Command to talk to about us flying those B-25H's back to the States. We were in luck: the Commanding General, Harold Alexander, was in his office and agreed to see Terry and hear his proposal.

While they talked, I got directions to MacArthur's fabled mountain-top "Villa," as it is described throughout the South Pacific. The story going the rounds had it built by men who were supposed to be constructing an airfield. Another rumor claimed MacArthur never used the place because it was always socked in by clouds.

Terry's presentation went well. The General thought it an ingenious idea, good for morale, a simple solution to getting all those planes back to the States, and, best of all, did not require any ATC crews, now so involved with the Philippines invasion. He promised Terry a decision within a week.

It was our luck that the only shuttle back to Nadzab left during the afternoon, which meant we would have to eat dinner at Nadzab, could not dine at Hollandia. But there was time before the plane left for a look at MacArthur's "Villa." An MP permitted us to approach within a hundred yards—the General was aboard a ship in the Philippine Sea, he said—close enough to see that the "Villa" consisted of three pre-fab units fitted together and painted white. It looks down on Lake Sentani, and Mount Cyclops rises majestically in the rear, a huge waterfall cascading down its face. Visibility around the house seemed cloud-free and normal, but the top of Mount Cyclops was hidden by dark clouds. "Always is," the MP said.

Nadzab, November 11—General Alexander's aide contacted Terry today with good news. We can begin rounding up volunteers for the crews to fly the B-25s home. Each crew must consist of five men: a certified B-25 pilot; a second pilot qualified to fly relief; a navigator who has done celestial navigation; an engineer-radio operator. The fifth man must be qualified in one of those three disciplines.

Terry and I immediately began making the rounds of the tents, looking for men who will sign up. Orders authorizing the flight will not be cut until we have at least five qualified crews. As expected, we are not being overwhelmed with volunteers. Many say they will never willingly fly another military plane.

* * *

An old copy of *Stars and Stripes* found its way into the tent. Its headline reads: "FDR Wins Unprecedented 4th Term." He defeated Thomas Dewey with 53% of the popular vote.

Nadzab, November 15— Special Orders were issued today to those of us approved to fly the B-25s home. Terry and I managed to put 12 crews together—60 men willing to make the long flight, hopping from island to island in that little plane with only a single set of flight controls.

Terry and I are not on the same crew. My pilot is a Major Sevy from Utah, a veteran B-25 combat pilot.

We will be flown to Townsville, Australia, early next week to pick up our planes.

Tontouta Airport, New Caledonia, November 20—I met this day in New Guinea, followed it to northern Australia, and saw its sun set in the Coral Sea off the west coast of New Caledonia. I am now in the dayroom of the transient officers barracks at Totouta Airport, 30 miles from Noumea. I AM ON MY WAY HOME!

I'm tempted to shout it from the stage of the outdoor movie theatre, if only to an audience of swirling bats. It is long past midnight but I feel I must keep saying it to make sure everyone knows. It is not a mistake! I am not an escapee. But I am fearful of shutting my eyes.

* * *

The C-47 left Nadzab at dawn, flying to Townsville by way of a fuel stop at Port Moresby. It then followed the Great Barrier Reef south along Queensland's east coast. We were on the ground at Townsville in time for lunch but the B-25s were still being serviced for the long flight back. Terry and I borrowed a jeep for a quick tour of the wide, dusty streets of this now desolate, one-time bustling port city. The simple, frame houses all seemed to be supported by wooden stilts set in tins of oil. We were told this was meant to frustrate attempts by voracious ants from gaining entry.

* * *

The rattling, crackling sound of our B-25s two huge engines was somewhat unsettling on takeoff. To my ears, it was a continuous, orchestrated series of misfires, very unlike the thunderous, deep-throated rumbling roar of the four engines I heard from "Frenisi's" flight deck.

No matter. The plane was easily catapaulted into the washed-blue sky over the Coral Sea, and we soon found the easterly course to New Caledonia. Six-plus hours later, we found Tontouta Airfield below us. Our pilot, the major from Utah, did a showy, fighter-type drop-in landing. This "boxcar driver" was impressed.

I last visited Tontouta just one year ago minus four days, but this time I am traveling in a northeast direction, towards home, not west, to some jungle-covered island. What a difference the direction makes!

The "Paris" of the South Pacific did not beckon this night. A 60-mile roundtrip truck ride did not justify a one-hour stroll along Noumea's darkened, sewer-lined streets. The infamous, *Pacific* nightclub will continue to be known only in my imagination and memory.

Tomorrow: Fiji.

Nandi, Viti Levu, Fiji, November 21—This overnight hesitation at Nandi—for engine checks and refueling—is a repeat of my stopover coming out a year ago: an airbase—only visit. I do not regret its brevity this time; I only regret time not spent flying towards San Francisco.

The 4 1/2-hour flight getting here from New Caledonia was uneventful and literally unobserved by me. I spent all that time on the floor of the windowless, extremely noisy space directly behind and a level below the flight deck. I shared the floor with Barney, also a pilot, and the navigator, Davis. The radio operator-flight engineer, Flaherty, has his console there, and suffered our presence.

The only Fijians I encountered at Nandi, as on my last visit, were the dining room servers and the Officers Club bartender. There are 15 of us Americans, the crews of the three B-25s spending the night. We outnumber the New Zealanders assigned to Nandi. There are 9 other B-25s en route to Honolulu, and we have no idea where they are tonight. We're all flying the same course back but are free to set our own schedule.

Tomorrow we fly first to Canton Island, a 1200 mile hop; then to Christmas Island, for the night, another 1000 miles closer to home.

Christmas Island, November 21—Night has fallen, erasing the last trace of an horizon on this moonless, starless night. Only the pounding of the surf reassures me that we really are on an island, Christmas Island, not some remote planet. Canton, where we touched down briefy for refueling in the late morning, was equally desolate and alien. Even time was elusive: we had left Fiji at dawn on the 22nd, arrived at Canton six hours later—but a full day earlier! We had somehow lost 24 hours by crossing an imaginary line circling the globe!

En route between Canton and Christmas this afternoon Davis, the navigator, showed me the course he had plotted, a penciled line to the northeast which did not bisect so much as a reef—or come within sight of one—during the 1200 mile flight to Christmas. He extended the line with his ruler until it reached San Francisco. "Sixteen hours, on a tailwind," he said. Alas, our limit was about 12 hours!

Then Davis put his finger on a tiny speck a few hundred miles west of our course. "Howland Island," he said. "Where Earhart was headed when Noonan lost his way."

A little later, when I was having a turn at piloting, sitting there alone, staring at the glistening sea, lulled by the drone of the engines, I thought about the afternoon at Lae a couple of weeks ago when I stood at the end of that little dirt airstrip, staring out over Huan Gulf, searching the horizon in the direction of Howland, wondering, then as now, how Earhart's flight really ended . . .

John Rogers Field, Honolulu, November 22—The 6½-hour flight from Christmas seemed endless. As on so many missions, there was no way to check our progress except by the clock—no islands or reefs that looked familiar, no cloud formations one remembered, not even the faintest line on the horizon to confirm we were headed in the right direction until the last hour or so.

I did have a turn in the pilot's seat and for a time—only the navigator and I were awake—I was reminded of the hours Pete and I had kept watch over "Frenisi," returning from missions, while the others slept. Pete and I had much to talk about during those private hours but Davis and I did not, nor wanted to share our secret and private expectations as we neared the end of the journey home.

We were instructed to land at Honolulu's John Rogers Field, the Naval Air Station, since the Air Force's nearby Hickam was presently overwhelmed with caring for a squadron of the new and still secret B-29s.

Those we glimpsed on the adjacent field were the first any of us had ever seen. We thought it the most beautful airplane ever built.

* * *

We have been set free until 8:00 AM next Monday, four days from now. I've already had a long, hot shower and changed into my last pair of clean—if wrinkled—khakis. I write this while awaiting Davis to finish dressing. We intend to face Honolulu tonight.

Fairfield-Suisun Army Airfield, Calif., December 2—Our arrival here, this afternoon, was at 3:32 PM I saw it on the tower clock as we taxied by. Flaherty said we had only 20-minutes of fuel left. All of us still kind of misty-eyed after passing over Golden Gate.

* * *

No one crouched in the shadows to flutter a scarf when we departed Oahu last midnight. Only an anonymous voice in the headsets acknowledged our takeoff: "Aloha, eight-eight-five!"

The Major dutifully skirted blacked-out Honolulu in the climb to altitude. Punchbowl Crater was down there somewhere I knew, but since it no longer needed to hold a gravesite for me, I felt no obligation to seek out its shadows this night.

At the top of our swift spiral climb, we turned to an east-northeast course and began looking for the California coast, still 2,000 miles beyond the horizon. Diamond Head was already far behind us.

* * *

I endured the darkness and cold of the flight deck's back recesses for most of the next 13 hours. Sometimes I slept; mostly I thought of the week just past: the joy of that first day, tumbling from the bus into Honolulu's downtown multi-hued street crowds; of marveling at the streams of horn-blowing taxis and trucks and military vehicles; then finding the largest, most luxurious barbershop any of us had seen, entering and immediately claiming every vacant chair, only to discover that all the barbers were pretty young oriental girls, some undoubtedly of Japanese ancestry.

Mine, quietly, politely, speaking in an accented GI patois, asked where I had been, what I had done, and I answered briefly as possible, carefully avoiding use of the pejorative "Jap" word, as she snipped and shaved and brushed away the months of South Pacific patina.

On leaving, we were directed, with giggles, to a multi-storied building in the rear, should any of us desire a lengthy, head-to-toe body massage, including hot soaks and perfumed oil rubs and ice water dunks. Some of us did.

Terry and I re-established our Nadzab-based friendship and spent the week of sun-blinding afternoons swimming and surfing on Waikiki in the shadow of the Royal Hawaiian hotel, now crudely camouflaged in black and green; sipping cooling, fruited, rums and gins on palm-shaded, flower-banked terraces; slow-dancing moonlit nights, carelessly lost, in tiny clubs on darkened wharfs and narrow dead-end alleys where sometimes Terry and I were the only uniformed patrons.

All the nights ended, relentlessly, when our taxicab-chariot was rudely exchanged for a half-empty military bus, and we took the lonely, quieting ride along deserted, half-lighted tree-lined streets to the guarded gates of John Rogers Field.

My turn at piloting on the last leg of the flight home came during the exploding sunrise of December 1, one so cruelly bright the reds and yellows stung my eyes. I thought of Koror's sun, last September, lifting flaming from the Philippine Sea, shedding irridescent droplets of water as it ascended. Only Koror's sky-high rainbow, under which "Frenisi" silently glided, was missing.

The Major was at the controls, hours later, when Golden Gate Bridge began to come into focus on the horizon. I crowded for space at the small side window to glimpse the remembered shrine.

Standing at last on Fairfield's tarmac, I swallowed a small cry of joy and thankfulness. The slender embrace of hope and fear that held me safe all these lost months can now be loosened.

* * *

Terry and I leave in the morning for Chicago. By train. Then, two weeks of home leave.

Coda

Wisconsin, as I had always known and my father no doubt suspected, was not the "home" I longed for. Within days I repacked my B-4 bag and moved on to New York City. There, only Martha sensed my unease at still feeling apart from those I had been so anxious to rejoin. My uniform, my "Cap of Perseus," as Martha's friend, Ben Bellitt, called it, seemed to make me invisible to my friends. Everyone seemed anxious to make me feel I still "belonged." But of course I did not. Even Merce seemed remote, now so totally involved in his professional life.

At Martha's urging, I called the one person I had no obligation to call, hoping, I suppose, to learn that possibly we could still be friends. She agreed to see me, although ill and in bed. Few words were spoken; no notes were passed. I left when the silent room began to darken, knowing that we no longer had anything to say to one another.

In January, I was assigned to Ft. Logan, outside Denver, Colorado, a rehabilitation facility for flyers suffering from combat fatigue. I was sent there as a public relations officer and occasional pilot of the Commanding Officer's twin-engined Beechcraft. It was part of a plan worked out by Martha's friend, Merle Armitage, now a colonel in charge of reassigning returned flyers, to bring me back to New York City as soon as a post opened up.

I returned to New York in May on furlough and finally got to see the dances Martha's letters so eloquently described as they were being created: *Deaths and Entrances, Salem Shore, Appalachian Spring* and *Herodiade*.

I also got to meet a stunning new member of the Company known simply as "Yuriko," who, unbeknownst to me, had joined while I was overseas. I was told she had come to New York directly from a relocation center out west for Japanese aliens, having been interned with her parents even though she was born in the United States and was an American citizen. Unexplainably, Yuriko had never been mentioned by Martha in letters to me. I could only guess that Martha had, naively, been fearful of my reaction to meeting the "enemy," albeit in the guise of a beautiful young dancer. But, as Martha had intended, and hoped, Yuriko and I became friends.

On the second night of the performances, *Letter to the World* was presented, evoking bittersweet memories of the last time I had danced my small part so long ago, wondering if I would ever again know the thrill and excitement I felt then. What I had come to learn was that only the threat of death—the attack of a Zeke fighter, exploding anti-aircraft shells under the wing, being lost a thousand miles from our island home in a starless night sky—could bring the same intensity of feeling.

Later that week in May, a telegram from Fort Logan informed me that I was eligible for discharge from the Air Force and should return there immediately.

* * *

Martha's last letter to me, dated June 5, 1945, told me she had received a card the Air Force sent former employers of servicemen being discharged. She said there was an initialed postscript at the bottom of the card reading:

"Plié inspected and O.K."

The plié was "O.K." enough, Martha thought, for me to rejoin the Company in the fall for one more season; but not good enough, we both knew, for me to ever be a "real" dancer, only a Spectator . . .

Log of Combat Missions

November 1943–September 1944

Date	Target	Air Time
1943	(*From Guadalcanal*)	
11/27	Bonis	7:30
11/29	Kieta	5:15
12/3	Bonis	6:00
12/5	Tsirogei (Sortie)	5:00
12/10	Tsirogei (Sortie)	4:10
12/12	Poporang	6:45
12/14	Sohana Is.	6:20
12/16	Bonis	6:40
1944	(Rest Leave: Auckland, N.Z., January 11–22)	
	(*From Munda, New Georgia*)	
2/14	Rabaul (Rapopo)	8:45
2/15	Rabaul (Borpop)	7:00
2/18	Rabaul (Vunakanau)	6:40
2/21	Rabaul (Lakunai)	6:50
2/27	Rabaul (Vunapope)	6:15
3/6	Kavieng	8:10
3/8	Rabaul (Rapopo)	6:40
3/10	Rabaul	6:20
3/14	Rabaul (Keravat)	6:50
3/16	Rabaul (Vunakanau)	6:40
3/18	Rabaul	6:15

Date **1944**	Target *(From Munda, New Georgia)*	Air Time
3/20	Rabaul (Vunakanau)	7:00
3/22	Kahili	5:30
4/6	Dublon Is., Truk (from Nissan Is.)	10:30
4/25	Dublon Is., Truk (from Nissan Is.)	12:35
	(From Admiralty Island)	
5/6	Woleai	8:45
5/8	Biak	10:35
5/12	Biak	10:45
5/14	Biak	9:30
5/16	Biak	10:00
5/18	Biak	10:00
5/24	Biak	9:30
5/27	Biak	10:30
	(Rest Leave: Sydney, Australia, June 1–30)	
7/3	Yap	13:10
7/4–5	Sorol Is.	11:00
7/10	Yap	13:00
7/15	Yap	12:20
7/22	Yap	12:30
7/27	Woleai	9:45
8/2	Woleai	9:30
8/6	Yap	13:00
8/8	Yap	12:45
	(From Wakde)	
8/25	Palau	9:00
8/29	Pelieu	9:15
9/2	Palau (Koror)	9:00
9/4	Palau	10:30
9/8	Halmahera	10:00
9/13	Halmahera	10:00
9/15	Halmahera	10:00
9/18	Ceram (Hardekoe)	9:00

Suggested Readings

American Caesar: Douglas MacArthur, William Manchester (Little, Brown, 1978)

The Army Air Forces in World War II, vols. IV, V, & VII (University of Chicago, 1958)

But Not in Shame, John Toland (Random House, 1961)

The Cactus Air Force, Thomas J. Miller, Jr. (Harper & Row, 1969)

The Coast Watchers, Eric A. Feldt (Oxford Univ., 1946)

Day by Day: The Forties, Thomas M. Leonard (Facts on File, 1977)

Eleanor and Franklin, Joseph P. Lash (Norton, 1971)

Fodor's New Zealand (1987)

Fodor's South Pacific (1990)

Greatest Fighter Missions, Edward Sims (Harper, 1962)

Growing Up in New Guinea, Margaret Mead (Morrow, 1933)

Guadalcanal, Richard B. Frank (Random House, 1990)

High Honor, S. Leuthner & O. Jensen (Smithsonian, 1989)

Hirohito: The War Years, Paul Manning (Dodd, Mead, 1986)

Last Flight, Amelia Earhart (Putnam, 1937)

Log of the Liberators, Steven Birdsall (Doubleday, 1973)

Lonely Vigil, Walter Lord (Viking, 1977)

The Long Rangers: A Diary of the 307th Bombardment Group, Sam Britt, Jr. (Baton Rouge, LA, 1990)

MacArthur's Navy, Edwin P. Hoyt (Jove, 1991)

Micronesia, A Travel Survival Kit, Glenda Bendure & Ned Friary (Lonely Planet, 1988)

Munda Trail, Eric Hammel (Orion-Crown, 1989)

New Lives for Old, Margaret Mead (Morrow, 1956)

Our Jungle Road to Tokyo, Robert L. Eichelberger (Viking, 1950)

The Pacific: Then and Now, Bruce Bahrenburg (Putnam, 1971)

The Pacific Islands (revised), Douglas L. Oliver (Doubleday Anchor, 1961)

Pacific Sweep, William N. Hess (Doubleday, 1974)

Papua New Guinea, A Travel Survival Kit, Tony Wheeler (Lonely Planet, 1988)

Return to Paradise, James Michener (Random House, 1951)

Solomon Islands, A Travel Survival Kit, David Harcombe (Lonely Planet, 1988)

South Pacific Handbook, David Stanley (Moon Publications, 1979–1986)

Tin Roofs and Palm Trees, Robert Trumbull (Univ. of Washington, 1977)

Up the Slot, Samuel L. Walker (Inter-Collegiate Press, 1984)

U.S. Naval Operations in World War II, vols. V, VI, & VIII, Samuel E. Morison
     (Little, Brown, 1949)

World War II: Island Fighting, Rafael Steinberg (Time-Life, 1977)

World War II: The Rising Sun, Arthur Zich (Time-Life, 1977)

About the Author

DAVID ZELLMER became an Air Cadet in October of 1942—within days of giving his final performance as a member of the Martha Graham Dance Company. Forty-six missions and 12 months later, he returned to the United States to begin life anew. Eventually he went on to pursue a career in broadcast journalism as a writer and producer at CBS News. This is his first book.